LIEUT. WARREN H. MILLER, U. S. N. R.

For Seven Years Editor of *Field and Stream*

THE SPORTSMAN'S WORKSHOP

By
WARREN H. MILLER
**Author of Camping Out, Camp Craft, The Boy's Book of
Hunting and Fishing, etc.**

Illustrated by Barse Miller

ISBN-13: 978-1514301876
ISBN-10: 1514301873

Printed in U.S.A

Contents

List of Illustrations

5

LIST OF ILLUSTRATIONS

THE
SPORTSMAN'S WORKSHOP

CHAPTER I

Equipping the Shop

I SUPPOSE that back in the mind of each one of us there lurks a certain dark and obscure scheme, carefully concealed from the female members of the family, that *some* day we are going to grab a room—that small one off the upper hall will answer—and in that room we are going to establish a shop, a sportsman's den, where none of the conquering sex may enter. We visualize that shop in our mind's eye. We long for it, yearn for it, especially what time the various repair jobs on tackle, camp gear, and shooting irons become pressingly urgent, and we have to upset the kitchen and get in everybody's way to make them. We curse our way through these jobs, hunting up lost tools, trying to make a chair do the work of a regular bench, using feet, hands, and teeth to take the place of the vise that should be there right to hand —you all know all about it. "Ain't it the truth," brothers?

Some of us have been bold enough to assert a modicum of masculine authority and seize said room, to have and to hold. There is no escaping the fact that camp gear *will* come back from the hunt shot to pieces, reels and rods go on the fritz, guns get rusty and in vast need of taking apart and overhauling throughout. We just *must* have a place we can call our own to do these things in.

Let me describe you my ideal of a shop, and see if the picture is attractive enough to make a struggle for: A small room, with two windows in it, and eight by ten feet in dimensions or even less is plenty. In it I want, first of all, a place to work *on*, and for this I do not think you can equal the ordinary deal kitchen table with stout legs, compared to any carpenter's contraption whatever. You want a place to stow your legs under and to work in comfort while the old pipe sozzles in its bowl and the snow and sleet are beating against the panes outside. As you work you dream over the camps and tramps of the season before and plan for the ones to come when spring again wakens the forest to life.

This table, then, may be 3 feet 6 inches long by 2 feet wide, standing 2 feet high, with plain board top. On it, at your right, is a husky vise, with anvil and horn; a vise that will hold gun barrels, woodwork being planed, and the like. At the left end is a little fellow for holding fine work, small gun parts, reel pinions, fish-hooks being converted into artificial baits, delicate work of all kinds. The only other fixture on the table is a small lathe head, with chucks and face plate, set well back to the left, and with a round belt going to a wheel and treadle under the table. This will be for turning small parts, rod-winding, and various polishing jobs. It is all the lathe you will ever need.

EQUIPPING THE SHOP

In front of the table goes a bench, an ordinary low laundry bench—*not* a chair. Why? Because you cannot beat a bench as a place on which to lay long pieces of timber being sawed, while you hold down with a knee; and, moreover, you can shift along it with ease to front your job and set hammers and tools beside you on it, where they will be handy to pick up when wanted and not cluttering up the surface of the table where the work is. Am I right?

All right: On the table, at the back, and pushed flat against the wall, we have to have a flat cabinet, say 28 inches wide by 36 inches high and 9 inches deep. This cabinet has a row of drawers, one above the other on each side, deep drawers, 6 inches by 8 inches, for holding our sets of tools and materials for mending and making camp gear and tents, the leather work on straps and moccasins; a drawer for reloading tools for rifle and shotgun cleaning implements, broken shell extractors, etc.; a drawer for your rod-winding and repairing materials, and parts for making baits and lures; a couple of drawers on each side, as flat as trays, for holding nails, screws, rivets, grommets, and all those small odds and ends that we men keep against the day they may come useful.

The space above the drawers and in between them is kept clear and open for hanging saws, hammers, wrenches, planes, metal-working tools, brace and bits—those tools that we have found from long usage are just what we need and no more.

Now, as to tools. This is going to be a joy shop, a place where the philosophical sportsman can sit him down and enjoy the pleasure of seeing good work grow under his eyes with *good* tools. Nothing is more aggravating and nothing induces the furious cussword more readily than to see good material for well-planned work being spoiled by dull, weak, or inept tools, things to work with that not only do not do what we ask of them, but spoil the material by being too large, too small, too dull, or out of order, like a sticking saw. We are going to avoid all that and enjoy our winter evenings, while all the time dreams of what we shall do with all this in the woods next season float through the mind.

A long experience in making gear of all kinds for outdoor use has shown me that the sportsman's workshop needs but few tools, and most of these specialties. But they must all be good, the best; steel that *is* steel, that no carpenter would be ashamed to use in his business. That refers even to hammers, that useful tool so often slighted. It will be of good steel, well balanced, with a hard, flat face that will stay flat and not glance off the next nailhead. Of wood saws we will need three: a first-class cross-cut, ditto compass, ditto back-saw. Then we want a metal-cutting saw for the shootin'-iron bench, and the tale of toothed help-meets is done. Of planes, two: an iron jack-plane for edging and smoothing, about a foot long across the flat, and a small, keen hand plane for little jobs. A good ratchet brace comes next, and such drills and bits and metal-working twist drills as we need for the various jobs that come up. Buy as you go along; they will accumulate fast enough! A breast

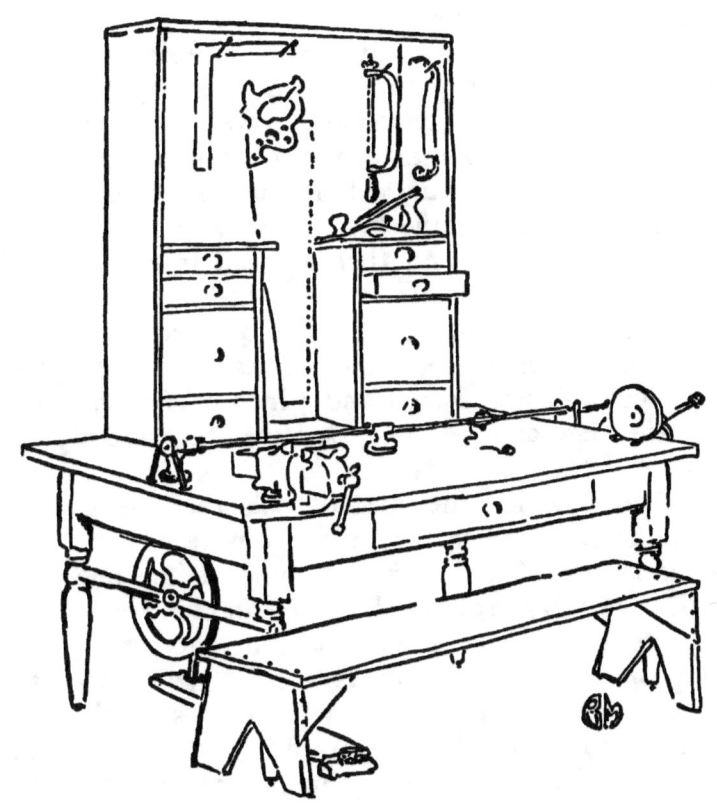

TABLE, BENCH AND CABINET FOR A SPORTSMAN'S
WORKSHOP

drill is a wrist saver not to be despised. I for one vote for it and repeat. See that it has a chuck that will hold metal drills.

Of screwdrivers you will need quite a set, from the big fellow that can be used as a pry and will turn an obstinate quarter-inch screw stuck fast in oak, to a little slender one that will take out the smallest thing on your reel or your rifle mechanism. On the pliers list come first a heavy one with good side cutting jaws, and then a small fellow, also of steel, with hatched face to hold the smallest hook, and then one round-nosed one for turning things. Half a dozen files—rounds, flats, and triangles. Two cold chisels, 8-inch and 4-inch. That is about all the regular line tools; perhaps you have a good many of them already.

And now for the special tools that we woodsmen find indispensable in our business. In tentmaking the ⅜-inch brass grommet is the one that will give universal satisfaction—and you will need 'em to stick in here and there in pack gear, too. A grommet set for it costs about $3, and consists of a die anvil and a punch with long, smooth nose, which curls the thimble of the grommet over its ring. A single blow of the hammer sets the grommet ring fast in the hem of your tent, where it grips the cloth tight, and is finished over in a neat round hole. Beats the scheme of trying to turn the thimble edge with a big nail out of sight, makes a round hole for your rope to pull through, and holds the cloth like grim death.

For leather working we want two kinds of rivets: the tubular, with a blunt cone punch to set them, and the split, which comes in small boxes, with a holding tool to seize the head of the rivet while you put it on the spot and hit it a crack with the hammer, which drives it through the leather. Turning it over, the points are started apart by a blow on a small round bar like the shank of a screwdriver, and then flattened out with a finishing thwack of the hammer face.

The shoemakers use a sort of lever punch for setting tubular rivets. I have one, but never got much satisfaction out of it, and generally prefer to drive my rivet into the leather and meet it on the other side with the set punch, a single blow on which curls over the edges of the tube so that they roll down on the leather and hold. A third type of rivet is the common copper one with copper washer, used for big strap corners where a heavy strain is to come on straps or woodwork and you need something to hold till the leather breaks first. This type requires a punch to make the hole first, which punch is also used in making buckle-holes in straps. It is a sort of pliers with a steel $\frac{1}{8}$-inch punch and a brass seat on the lower jaw. For larger holes, particularly through canvas in setting grommets, a plain $\frac{5}{16}$-inch punch that one hits with a hammer, with a block of wood underneath for anvil, is a tool that you cannot make camp gear without. A small cousin of the grommet is the eyelet, that little brass fellow that you see in boots for the lacings to run through. An exceedingly useful critter in leather is the eyelet; in canvas he will not hold well enough to be worth setting in. Better use a grommet instead. A combination tool for punching and setting the eyelet is sold at the hardware stores for about $2.

Three or four awls, straight and curved, a hank of stout twine with brass needles attached, a patent hand sewing awl, a ball of linen shoemaker's thread, a blob of beeswax, and a ball of cotton twine, make up your outfit for tent and moccasin repairing. The sewing is best done with two needles at once, pushing through from opposite sides and so making a double lock stitch along the seam. Using the awl to punch holes, almost any moccasin seam can be repaired that way. For leather work where you cannot get at the inside a special tool comes, called the "hand sewing awl," handled by most sporting goods houses and hardware stores. It consists of a stout needle with a spool of twine on the handle. You punch it through the leather and pull out again. A length of thread is left inside. Putting your hand into the moc, you guide this thread through the needle point loop for the next punch, and so get a lock stitch. How many perfectly good mocs have we thrown away, simply because they had a hole in the sole up near the toe where they could not be gotten at with a needle! This tool will save $'s in repairing such soles!

For further tent and leather-working tools, add a stout, sharp pair of shears; a sharp knife, with a bevel edge for cutting leather and making moccasin thong strips, and a small ¼-inch chisel for making holes where an overhand seam of flat rawhide is to go. It may not seem that there is so very much of leather and canvas work to do in the sportsman's workshop—but just look over your camp gear! Here are burn-holes and tears in the tents, straps off and rivets torn out in duffle bags and pack harness, mocs with leaky seams and holes in the soles—no end of it to be fixed up, so that you will hit the woods with outfit in good order next time.

And then, making new stuff! We all plan new tents, new packs, new sleeping rigs. We lost our hunting knife, perhaps, and if we just could make a good sheath, there are plenty of fine butcher knives at one tenth the price that will answer just as well—*if* they had a sheath! And then that big ax of ours has never had a sheath of its own, having gone along with its edge swathed in gunnysack. Why not make a real sheath for it this winter?

I should say that the metal-working part of the shop comes next in importance. The cook outfits get out of repair, lose their bails and wire, need rivets, get battered and bent, and the guns and reels have a way of accumulating rust and dirt that passes belief. I would rather blow myself on that big vise, for a starter. There is a very good one with 2½-inch jaws, opening about five inches, with an anvil and horn on the body end. Blessed tool! There is hardly a metal job in the shop that does not get into or on that vise at some time or other. For metal rivets, a store of the ordinary round-head soft iron rivet will be in one of those tray drawer pockets, and is requisitioned for cook kit repairs, also for new work like tinkering up a camp stove that you swear is the best bet ever, or making a new-fangled camp grate out of a broiling spider. Then the hardware stores are full of near-good camp utensils that have a foolish gadjet or handle sticking out somewhere, and this the metal bench removes and you are the proud possessor of something new and good to hit the trail with next time.

You try that salt-water reel. Gummed fast; its drag sets itself; its take-apart doohickie is fast with green rust; it needs taking all to pieces and each part cleaned, oiled, and vaselined. Out come the screwdrivers, the oil can, and the kerosene dropper, and you go after him. The fresh-water reels are not apt to suffer much from this sort of thing; their troubles are mostly working loose or having been squeezed in a pack until the frame is skewed or out of round, when you take it apart and fix the frame at the metal bench.

A general overhauling of the guns finds the actions inside caked with old grease, rust, powder corrosion; and that new sight that you intended putting on has come in by mail. With the metal bench and the oils and screwdrivers a happy evening is spent, ending with the satisfactory and smooth clicking of a clean gun. In these days of ten-cent cartridges it more than pays to save the shells and do your own reloading. Both the Ideal and Winchester people have new tools now for the big high-power rifles. A Bunsen burner and stand for it is the first special tool I would want. A very good substitute for it is one of those little cast iron blue flame gas burners with level wings to set pots on. Either of them is to be connected to your gas tap with a length of flexible hose, and you thus have a clean, safe means for melting lead, soldering, drawing temper, or heating iron to a bending heat. For a forging heat you would need a pot forge of some sort, with bellows.

Another special tool which belongs in this section is one of those small emery grindstones, operated by hand, with gearing. One of these will cost as little as a dollar, and has a screw clamp for attaching on the table edge. It will save much weary filing and hand sharpening; for with it rough edges are put on axes, great and small; on tools and knives; and jobs of taking off metal to get a smooth fit are ground down on it. Another "special" is that bullet ladle supplied by the reloading companies. This has a tube nozzle so that it can be faced on the mould and then inverted, when you get a pressure pour, which means a good deal in averting spoiled and bubbly bullets. A few C-clamps for compressing gun springs, emery and crocus cloths of various degrees of fineness, and you have done with specials for the metal bench.

In general reloading I find several extras which are worth while. A shell rack which will hold fifty of them is one of these. You can make it by simply boring holes of the size to take the shell base. Mine is a two-story one, with the upper board perforated so that the shells are gripped at mid-height. In either case it prevents that aggravating annoyance of a row of shells being tipped over while filled with powder or shot charges and no wads in. It goes without saying that shell loading proceeds quickest when all the separate operations are done in batches, all powdered, wadded, shotted, primed, decapped, etc., at one time. Something to hold the shells firmly is the needful, especially during the later operations. Another special tool is a metal rammer. Mine is made of brass. The wooden one furnished will not stand much tapping with your mallet. You are supposed to use the cup of your hand, but this becomes irksome long before fifty shells are done, let alone a hundred of them. No; a brass rammer and a light mallet make the ideal combination.

Passing on to the fishing-tackle section of the shop, the first thing wanted will be a rod-winding appliance. Two wooden uprights with V notches make the simplest combination that can be built. If one of these is fixed permanently at the right-hand end of the table, to the rear, it can be used very effectively, turned by hand or with the little hand emery wheel aforementioned, by running a light tape belt over the wheel and around a wooden flanged wheel slipped over the rod ferrule. This is not so complicated as it sounds. One size wheel is enough, and it is provided with a set of bushings to fit snugly on the male ferrules of your own rods. The proper bushing for the particular rod makes the wheel available for use. I find that the left-hand V upright may as well remain fixed, too, and on the bench is a movable rest with half-round adjustable support, which is to be set up alongside the place where the actual winding is being done.

A more elaborate rod winder is the lathe head aforementioned. It is nothing more than the ordinary small polishing wheel head, sold for a few dollars in the hardware stores, and has a chuck big enough to hold any small work or the end of a rod section. A V-notch upright and a rest complete the outfit as before. This lathe head is run by a round belt running down through holes in the table to a large grooved wheel, with treadle fixed to a diagonal brace bolted to the left-hand pair of table legs. Those who want both a lathe and a rod winder may well consider putting in such a fixture.

This sketch covers in general the indoor activities of the shop. It is perfectly capable, however, of building you a fishing and gunning skiff, a canvas-decked sailing canoe, a dog kennel, or any other large wooden construction requiring more room in which to lay out and build. Mine has turned out all these delectable commodities, affording me many weeks of carefree vagabondage out in the great open. The boats were built down in the cellar, with part of the shop tools moved down there for the time being. The dog houses were put up right in the shop and eased out of its door—after the alarming discovery that they would just "make it" by taking the door itself off its hinges! The shop is always busy, especially after the strenuosities of the summer and fall camping trips, when everything comes in more or less frazzled. Who shall say that the pleasure of renewing the vigor of those war-worn commodities and of designing and making newer and better ones does not bring the outdoors indoors, an aura of the piney woods and the open waters surrounding each one of them, and the ponderable odor of fly dope and wood-fire smoke filling the shop with the aroma of the woods!

As perhaps one of the first activities of *your* shop will be building its own cabinet, I give here a sketch from which a design, modified to suit the original preferences of the builder, can be made. And, as prices of ordinary tools have soared to unheard-of heights, I give here a list of the present hardware-store costs of *good* tools comprising the selection suggested in the first part of this article.

Hammer, steel, best quality	$1 66
Saw, cross-cut, Disston	3 45
Saw, compass	55
Saw, back, 16-inch	1 70
Saw, hack, metal	75
Ratchet brace	3 85
Bits	40
Jack plane, iron, 12-inch	3 75
Hand plane, small	1 15
Pliers, side cutting, large	1 25
Files	25
Large steel vise, anvil, and horn	5 85
Small vise	1 25
Breast drill	2 25
Leather hand sewing awl	60
Grommet set	2 50
Punches, set punches, etc.	35

1. Rucksack and Bed Roll
2. Vreland-Forester Tent
3. Cree Three-bar Snow Shoes
4. The Author's Wall Tent
5. Three-pot Tent Stove
6. Tarp for Eating Table, 2½ Lbs.

CHAPTER II

Tent Making

THE trade of Omar has certain subtle satisfactions for the male animal which makes its practice peculiarly agreeable, even while the actual labor of tent-making is going on. Man is never more at home with himself than when trying to make a tent of sorts. It is the *women* who have got us into this prodigious tangle of house-owning, house-building, house-furnishing, and then wasting the better part of our lives paying for and repairing these undesirable possessions! The tent whispers to us of emancipation, freedom from all that, a home that costs comparatively nothing, that is better without *any* furniture, and that has no fixed abiding place. Truly that Persian poet was right when he objected to the palace the sultan had presented to him, on the score that it could not be moved!

I suppose that in thirty years of camping out there is hardly a type of tent that I have not used or lived in at one time or another. It is an incredible list—teepee, wall tent, shelter tent, forester, miner, handy, Nessmuk, canoe, canoe cockpit, lone hiker's, snow, Appalachian, tarp-and-canoe, wedge, Esquimo, "perfect," "Dan Beard," or "Campfire"—ye red gods, what a list! Six of these

I designed myself, and one, the "forester," has been appropriated by the sporting-goods houses without even naming it so as to give its inventor a modicum of credit. Ah, well-a-day; would that I, too, could grab the cash and let the credit go!

But of them all, I have come to boil down my preferences to just three, and the first of these is the oldest and best—would you believe it, none other than the wall tent! For general camping a little one weighing 4½ pounds and covering 6 by 5 feet in area by 6 feet high is the one that goes oftenest with me. The year before the war I thought I had designed perfection in tents by a modified "Handy" of the same floor area, but with a dormer window on the rear slant of the roof. But that dormer was a nuisance to rig, and used up as much canvas as would make the rear roof grow to a complete wall tent with the desired window in the back wall. A window I *would* have—something big enough to keep the tent from turning into an oven in the daytime and to see out of when at work inside. So my final tent was a wall tent with 14-inch walls, a sod cloth run around inside, roof 4½ by 6 feet long, a scrim front sewed to the door all around in front, and the cover flap of the door openable to make a veranda in front. This tent is always pitched by a ridge rope run from tree to tree, its bottom pegged down with ten stakes, and its eaves guyed out to the surrounding bushes, or stakes if there are no saplings handy. One stands up in it easily; there is room for three to sleep in a pinch; it is easily warmed by a small cylindrical stove, and to get more head-room we gambrel the roof with a couple of withes bent over the ridge rope inside, where they spread out the upper slant to increase the head-room to shoulder width. The stove for it is a mere shell of sheet iron, in which slip three of those aluminum fireless cooker pots, forming a circle between them, and about 9 inches in diameter by 6 inches deep. This shell is of 28-gauge sheet steel, 4 inches longer than the pots, to accommodate a steel folding fry pan and a nest of plates in the lower end. The whole thing goes into a canvas bucket and packs atop my bedding and tent roll, carried vertically by a shoulder harness like an army pack. The stove has a swinging door at the lower end and a come-out for an elbow and a 24-inch length of 2½-inch pipe. The elbow takes the smoke out through the tent wall, and the riser carries it well clear of the roof. I never could see the use of a long stove pipe. A well-managed fire in the stove requires little piping to make it draw.

This tent is my favorite for cold weather camping, and goes with me on all hunting trips and all early fishing trips in the North where the nights are "plumb" cold.

The second survivor of all that list of tents is a shanty tent, with net sides and front and a detachable cloth side to snap on as a windshield. It covers 6 by 5 feet in area and weighs 3½ pounds. It is used for mid-summer camping, particularly beach camping, where your principal aim is to keep cool and escape mosquitoes and flies. It puts up with two 4½-foot poles and two 2-foot stakes at the rear corners. To these the four corners of the roof are tied, and ropes then led out to form corner guys. The net bar is staked down all around, and if there is a cold wind the extra cloth side is snapped on. For both woods camping after bass in June and September and all beach camping for salt-water fish, it fills the bill, is cool and airy in the daytime and full of the all-outdoors at night. The most refreshing thing to sleep in ever!

The third tent is the laziest of all, and is used for lone hiking trips. It weighs 2½ pounds, all told, and includes a canvas pocketed stretcher bed weighing nine ounces and a tarp 6 by 9 feet, weighing two pounds, including 30 feet of ridge rope. This tent sleeps and camps *one* very comfortably indeed. I pitch it by cutting two long, slender poles, using the bottom lengths of seven feet from each for the sides of the stretcher bed, and the rest to make up two pairs of shears, over which the ridge rope is run. The bed poles are lashed to the shear legs about a foot above the ground, and the tarp is spread over the ridge rope, pegged down flat to windward, and the front edge guyed out to form a veranda, under which a fire can be built in front of the cot in rainy weather. A mosquito canopy hangs down over face and shoulders at night, hung by a string from the ridge rope. A very comfortable little tent for lone hiking or going with a party where each has his own tent and cooking gear.

These are my three favorite tents; you probably have your own. To make any and all of them, certain principles of tent design must be respected. No strain must come on any part of the tent except the seams. Up these the stress of guy ropes and pegs runs to the rafter or ridge rope. Tent

THE HANDY TENT

THE AUTHOR'S MIDGET WALL TENT

duck, eight-ounce, is now around forty cents a
yard, but bids fair to go lower. The department
stores do not carry brown khaki, but you can get
a bolt of it from any of the big outfitters or from
such manufacturers as the John H. Meyers Com-
pany, of Fourth Avenue, New York. Most of it
is in 30-inch widths. For general tent-making
ordinary eight-ounce duck is good enough, but a
bit heavy. The waterproof brown "army" tent-
ings weigh about six ounces to the running yard,
some four. Paraffined linen or cotton, usually dyed
green, runs about three ounces to the yard, and now
costs somewhere around 60 cents; used to be 38
cents when I was making my own tents. This,
too, can be bought from the outfitters, and comes
36 and 40 inches wide. It is best gored down the
middle with a single fold, as you will want your
pegs nearer than 30 inches. The usual width between seams is 18 inches.

The ordinary house sewing machine is perfectly capable of making tents, packs, duffle bags,
sleeping bags, and all the usual canvas camp gear.
It will sew anything it can drive its needle through,
an incredible number of thicknesses, even five,
having gone under the foot of my machine. It
does, however, want a stout needle and stout
thread; 40 cotton brown is best. The needle is the
stoutest the machine will take, something that will
punch down through the toughest canvas corner,
even if you have to aid it with your hand on the
wheel for the first few stitches. I usually pin my
seams with a three-quarter-inch single overlap and
run the upper seam first just inside the edge of the

goods, taking out pins as I come to them. Then turn over and do the other edge, which goes much easier.

In cutting for the dimensions it is a good plan to make a miniature of the tent of stiff white paper to scale, particularly if it is a complicated one. Then from the diagonal edges take off the dimensions with an architect's scale—without which I would not be happy. In cutting for a complicated tent, like a snow or a handy, it is well to outline the entire tent with a skeleton string affair, run from poles and tacks in the floor to represent corner pegs. The cloth can then be cut to meet the strings, allowing two inches overlap for seams and hems, and the whole tent built with pins every six inches to hold it together. When just right and with overlap enough allowed on all seams, take it apart, section by section, and sew each one up on the machine. Then assemble the sections until the entire tent is done.

For a wall tent the roof is to be made first. In my small one the roof was a rectangle 9 by 6 feet, sewed up out of two 40-inch-wide lengths of paraffined muslin, with one-inch laps down the center of each gore. It was then hemmed all around. The walls were next gotten out, 16 inches high by 6 feet long, and hemmed along the bottoms. The tops were then sewed inside the lap of the roof hems, so that the latter would project out an inch and leave a hem for grommet holes for the side-wall guys. The two ends were cut and sewed and finally run in under both end hems of the roof. Grommets were then put in at the ends of each seam, and I then had a plain wall tent—with no modern conveniences—hot as thunder in the daytime and breathy at night, for paraffined muslin will not pass air through its weave. So I set it up and cut out a two-foot triangular window in the peak of the rear wall, filling it with fine-mesh scrim. The piece cut out hangs down in clear weather, and can be hauled up under a hood run out on the rear ridge rope in cold, blowy seasons. I find that a foot length of triangular hood stretched out on the ridge rope from the sides of the window will shield it from rain. For a door I wanted first, a sill a foot high, to keep sand and dirt from being tracked into the tent and keep out small visitors while I was away in the woods. The door could be made about four foot six to the top and be eighteen inches wide before running into the peak of the roof, so this much canvas was cut out and added to, with long, flaring diagonals, so that it would grow to a respectable shade at some four feet from the tent. I did not sew up the remainder except above the flap, where it should be tightly waterproof. There are times when the whole front of the tent should be open to let in the warmth and cheer of the camp fire. The sill, then, was made so it could be unlaced from the grommets at its edges and the whole thing turned back.

Now, in fighting black flies, punkies, and mosquitoes I have come to learn that no net front except one sewed to the tent all along its inside edges is worth a whoop. The one for this tent was cut with a much wider angle than the roof peak, so that it would fall in easy folds, with a foot of lap below the sill. Lifting this, one could get inside easily, or it could be raised like a curtain so as to let in the fire heat unobstructed.

Except for the ridge rope, which should be of stout ⅜-inch cotton, there is no need for the additional weight of anything heavy for the wall guys. I use a hank of Banks line, such as codfish are caught on, a green braided line ⅛-inch in diameter, and 100 pounds strong. Six-foot lengths of this are ample for guy ropes, and very light. For peg ties the least aggravating and lightest are short two-foot lengths of common brown tape. Rope is mighty apt to kink and make the hardest of knots after a week of dampness in the duff, setting the knot like grim death. Tape unties more easily and is less bulky and heavy.

A final addition to this tent was a light edging of sod cloth eight inches wide, sewn around the bottom hem inside. It is of the lightest brown muslin, and is well worth its weight and bulk, for the sod cloth seals many an irregularity in the evenness of the forest floor and keeps out enterprising mosquitoes and black flies which would work in that way even through a considerable banking up of duff. More than once I have had a night spoiled by the unaccountable presence of mosquitoes or midges which had gotten in, heaven knows how, but the mystery was explained when the flasher showed a hollow under the bottom hem of the tent not completely filled with leaves. A sod cloth, held down by the lap of one's blanket bag, would have sealed that hole.

While on the important subject of insects, a

word on the bar material to keep them out: Ordinary mosquito netting is too coarse and too flimsy to be worth much in the woods. The hex-mesh bobbinet is proof against mosquitoes, but punkies and black flies go through it as through a tennis net. Cheese cloth will keep them out, but is stuffy and apt to draw its mesh so out of the true weave as to leave holes in places where *they* can get through. I have come to rely upon ecrou curtain scrim, which you can get in the upholstery department of most stores. This scrim is a fine mesh net, strong, and proof against mosquitoes and black flies.

To be free from annoyance from the pestiferous midge the only sure-fire is a canvas, totally closed tent. The forest air seeps through its weave at night, keeping it free from breathiness, and upon retiring you first close and tape the front flaps, which will have a loose strip of light cloth sewed down one edge to make a seal, and then with the flasher hunt down and slay each and every midge, black fly, and mosquito that may be found on the tent walls. Peace will then be yours for the rest of the night. It is the only tent I would take into a pest hole like the Adirondacks in summer.

Supposing that you have made the tent in ordinary eight-ounce duck, the first thing it will require when it comes off the machine and before grommeting will be waterproofing. I have used Nessmuk's lime-alum recipe for years. Ordinary duck tents waterproofed with it turn the most violent of thundershowers with ease, nor does the process add appreciably to the tent's weight. The recipe: "To ten quarts of water add ten

MOSQUITO NET FRONT SHELTER TENT

THE LONE HIKER'S STRETCHER-BED TENT

ounces of lime and four ounces of alum. Let it stand until clear. Fold tent and put in another vessel; pour the solution upon it, let it soak for twelve hours; then rinse in lukewarm rain water, stretch and dry in the sun, and the tent is ready for use." In practice I found that you had to heat the lime and alum solution over a fire to get the lime to slake. Perhaps it was the fault of the lime, or perhaps the alum kept it from slaking; anyway, if you see nothing doing with your lime, put it on the fire and she will soon start. An ordinary galvanized iron pail will hold ten quarts of water. The lime you get from any lumber concern. They will tell you where a building job is going on, and you hike over there and graft the ten ounces of quick lime where they are making fresh mortar. None of the drug store or hardware store limes are any good, being all slack. The alum you get at the drug store.

Nessmuk's direction to fold the tent I found would not do with new duck canvas. There is sure to be a large spot somewhere in the center of the folds entirely untouched by the liquor even after twenty-four hours' submersion. I always dip in the tent loose until the new, fresh cloth is wetted through and through. It can then be folded and capillary attraction will draw in the solution during the twelve hours' submersion. The chemical reaction is a double sulphate of lime and alum which gradually forms in the fibers. As this is insoluble in fresh water, it makes the tent waterproof for all slants over one in four. After a shower I find the tent roof with a sleek, soapy feel.

I have never tried the sugar-of-lead and alum process. It seems simple enough and is probably efficacious, as it is used by the Boy Scouts and many military organizations. One half pound each of alum and sugar-of-lead are dissolved in separate vessels containing four gallons of boiling rain water or other soft water. Allow to cool and settle until clear. After four hours' precipitation the clear liquors resulting of both solutions are poured together into a container holding the tent. You will note that it mixes to eight gallons, which will take care of quite a large tent. The cloth is thoroughly immersed in this pickle; just how long is not stated, probably twelve hours, to allow the chemical reaction of the alum and sugar-of-lead to fix itself into the fibers of the cotton. As it is insoluble by water, all that is now needed is to squeeze out the liquor, hang up tent and let dry, when the next rain that comes will run off down the surface of the cotton.

A third process that I have used a few times consists in dissolving a couple of cakes of grocery-store paraffin in a can of turpentine. To do this you must heat the "turps," either in a double boiler or back on some safe part of the kitchen stove, when it will readily dissolve the cut-up shavings of paraffin. A pint of "turps" will take up a brick of paraffin. I used this once on a very light tent made of American drilling. I painted it on with a flat brush, when the "turps" evaporated, leaving the drill impregnated with the paraffin. Then I set up the tent and turned a garden hose spray on her. She leaked in a number of spots.

These were repainted and the process kept up until it leaked nowhere. For another light tent I tried rubbing on the paraffin brick and following with a hot iron. This immediately drove in the paraffin. It proved water-tight, but stiff, and I am afraid that if used in cold weather that tent will crack. I was not much impressed with either of the paraffin processes on light goods. However, to make a light paraffined muslin tent, soak it in this solution after sewing up, and then stretch and dry. I would be inclined to shrink it first by soaking in the lime alum mixture, then dye, then finally paraffin.

As to dyeing tents, the plain white is easier to find in the woods, and also easier for others to find while you are away. The green and brown look less disreputable when dirty or mildewed, and we are not so conspicuous in the woods. I usually dye my tents brown with ordinary drug-store dyes. They should be well stirred while in the liquor boiling, for, if allowed to rest, the area of tent next the bottom will surely take on a darker color than the rest. Kephart gives a tan dye, home-brewed, of two pounds of white-oak bark dissolved in three and one-half gallons of boiling water. I never tried it, as the ten-cent dye was so much less trouble.

In conclusion, let me call your attention to two more tents that I still regard with approving memory. The first is the so-called "Handy" tent, a little totally enclosed fellow, 6 feet wide by 5 feet deep and 6 feet high. It has walls 18 inches high, a flat front of the same shape as the ordinary wall tent, but the side and back roof slants are triangles, sloping down to the walls from the single pole in front, with which it is put up. This tent is my favorite for very insecty country, and I prefer it made of plain single-filling department-store eight-ounce duck, so that I get a constant change of air during the night. Its roof is so steep that the lime-alum process waterproofs it completely. One can stand up to dress in the front part of it. With two cots inside it is ideal for a man and his wife. When three men sleep side by side on the floor its six feet of width gives them plenty of room, and the front face can be set out enough to accommodate their feet. Three friends of mine got away with this stunt once in the Adirondacks, so I know. I do not think that sportsmen in general are sufficiently acquainted with the excellencies of this little tent. Only one sporting goods house makes it, so far as I know.

The second tent is the good old "Forester." Lord love us, how time flies! It was just twenty years ago when I designed and built the first one of them. It is still my favorite cold-weather tent when I do not want to tote a stove. All its angles reflect the fire-heat rays down on the sleepers. It is very light, only six pounds, with hood, in ordinary department-store duck, and it is quickly put up with three poles cut in the nearest thicket. No thunderstorm has yet gotten through the steep roof of that tent, waterproofed by the home lime-alum process. A pack of houn' dawgs once pronounced it the warmest of all open tents, for out of three different selections before the same fire they all insisted in crowding into *my* tent. Could any flattery equal that? I give here the pattern of the hooded forester which anyone can make for himself. The original open type is the one grafted by the various manufacturers, but it is too leaky of good fire heat up the ridgepole and too vulnerable to driving rains to suit me. I put the hood on the second one I made, and have never sold anyone an open one.

People are always writing in, asking me, "What is balloon silk?" It is not silk at all, but a light-weight cotton fabric, close wove, of long fiber sea-isle cotton. It is used a good deal in fine yacht sails and in tent-making. Most of the big ship chandleries keep it in stock; also such houses as John Boyle, of Broome Street, New York. The weight is about four ounces to the yard.

Do not try to put eyelets in tent seams. The temptation to do so is great, particularly in lacing seams like a front. But the only thing which will hold is the grommet. And in fastening tapes where a strain is to come on them, like ridge tapes to go around an outside pole, give yourself plenty of anchorage to the tape, sew it all around the edges, and then diagonally across the rectangle in both directions.

CHAPTER III

Making Pack and Trail Gear

MOST of us who hit the trail to the woods frequently as the seasons roll by love to plan new gear or alter something already manufactured to "mold it nearer to the heart's desire," or else haunt the army-goods shop to pick up military stuff that, with a few changes, can be made into right serviceable woods equipment. Then, at the end of the year's camping, the winter nights see us mending and repairing this and that so that we may go afield bright and early next year with everything tip-top and good as new.

To do all this does not necessarily presuppose a shop, but it does require a few special canvas and leather-working tools, so as to make a job of work of whatever we set our hands to. First and foremost, the long-suffering family sewing machine needs two additions to make it worth while as a sewer of trail goods. It needs the stoutest needle the holder will take, and it needs sundry spools of at least twenty cotton weight. Your home sewing machine will sew anything it can drive its needle through, as much as five folds of canvas if necessary, but to do it it needs a stout needle with a big eye that will pass heavy thread. No light garment thread will answer. It may *look* strong as the seam comes off the machine and you give it a tentative yank, but sooner or later a strain will come on the very end of that seam and it will peel down and out like stripping a banana, and almost as easily. A seam of twenty brown cotton will hold almost anything in crosswise or longitudinal strain, but if by maneuvering the strap you can put a pull on it backward, over the head of the seam, so to speak— better put in a rivet as a stop, for this rivet will prevent the seam starting.

As to what can be sewed, you can tackle all grades of duck canvas with confidence, including the heavy brown ten ounce waterproof paraffined duck in four thicknesses; light leather, such as small buckle straps; army webbing straps of all sorts, and paraffined muslins for light tents, which will not leak through the seam holes if you use a light needle for them. This will include nearly all camp gear material except heavy leather, such as harnesses, tump straps, and moccasins. These latter may be worked by rivets and sewing with the hand leather sewing awl. This useful little tool costs sixty cents at the hardware stores, and has a set of needles of various fineness and curves in its hollow handle. Behind its chuck you will find a metal spool holding considerable heavy black sewing twine. The needle selected for the work is put in the chuck and the end of the thread slipped through its eyehole. You then punch through the two thicknesses of leather to be sewed and run the trailing thread through the loop left by the needle in withdrawing. This tail thread is caught and partly drawn into the hole as you pull tight, so that a two-thread seam is made, very strong and durable.

For special tools in camp gear making I would put first the ⅜-inch grommet set, a punch and die costing about $2.50, by which the thimble and ring of the ordinary brass grommet are turned over neatly and the ring made to seize the canvas tightly by the blow of the hammer. The toothed thimble is easier to set, but is a snare and a delusion when you want it to hold. A second tool would be the combination eyelet punch and set, which costs about $3, and punches holes in leather in which the small eyelet thimbles are then put and set fast by the tool. A most useful tool, in all sorts of places, in making packs, etc. A third tool is the belt-hole punch, costing about $1.50, for making holes where needed in your straps. You can make these holes with an awl and let the buckle tongue wear them full, but they will always give trouble in wet or cold weather, and are hard to undo compared to a regular belt hole.

All hardware, such as buckles, D-rings, snap hooks, tubular and washer rivets, etc., can be bought at any harness shop as you need them. Do not use the split rivets sold at the ten-cent stores. They either tear the canvas or fold up and pull out when a real strain comes on them. For setting tubular rivets a steel set punch with wide angle nose is the tool, and for making grommet holes in such obstinate stuff as ten-ounce paraffined brown duck get a $\frac{5}{16}$-inch steel punch.

This covers about all the tools really needed to

make and repair camp gear. When it comes to making new stuff, the list of things that a woodser wants is almost endless. You can make at home about everything sold in the outfitting stores. I have made my own canvas pails even, and had them come out waterproof and O. K. Nearly all of us have our own ideas of the ideal packsack, sleeping bag, cook kit, and war bag. In general the packsack may be classified in two main divisions: the square or pear-shaped bag of general knapsack type, and the long, cylindrical army type, starting from the duffle bag as its progenitor. Both ways are convenient and depend, I should say, on how you prefer to carry your tent and bedding. These two are the bulkiest of your trail articles, but the grub is always the heaviest and most compact, wherefore, to make your pack hang right, the place the heaviest thing is to go is the first consideration. My experience has been that if weight is packed high it tends to make the bag sag away from the shoulders and enormously increases the shoulder pressure and fatigue. If carried low the pack hugs in tight to the back. In both types, then, the heavy weights, ammunition, canned grub, and the like, should go in the bottom of the pack. Above them the tent, then war bags of small stuff, and finally the blanket roll. In the ideal pack both hips and shoulders should take part in sustaining the load. To do this in practice one puts one's fists or a rolled coat or sweater under the belt, where they will bear against the bottom of the knapsack, or, with the long type of pack like the Alaska

ARMY TYPE PACK THE DULUTH PACK

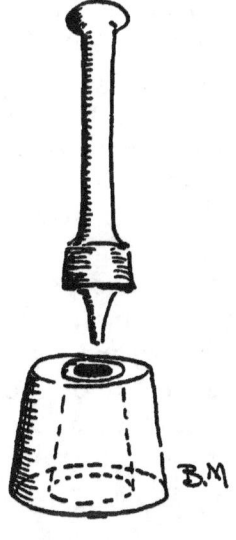

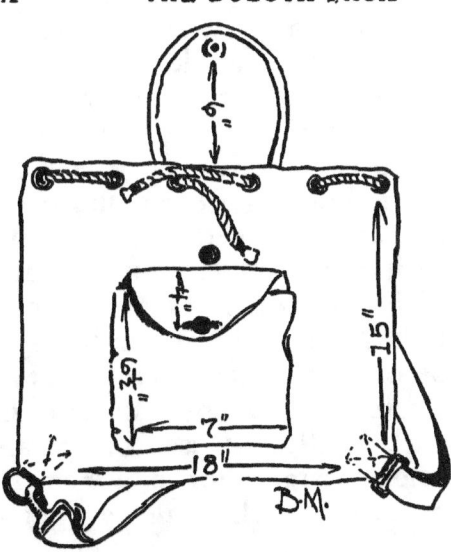

GROMMET SET RUCK SACK, FRONT VIEW

41

and the army, a hip brace is provided, with offsets and a strap which engage the hips, tipping the pack at a slight angle to the shoulders.

As to carrying strap fastenings, I am not yet convinced whether two straps set a few inches apart at a V with separate anchorage seams, or a D-ring with both straps coming from a single point, or a yoke curving around the neck, is the best. The two-strap is the staunchest, will not let the pack sling out of place on a sudden lean, and holds it flat across the back. The D-ring anchorage brings both straps crossing over the big muscles of the neck, but it tends to draw the pack to a peak like a bag, and it allows it to slue easily when one is thrown out of balance. The yoke fits snug, but is hot and likely to chafe. For the two-strap anchorage I use broad straps of thin, strong leather sewed down the canvas with D-rings at their tops. The carrying straps are riveted in these and have broad sliders of heavy leather on them which can be slipped into position over the shoulders, thus distributing the pressure and preventing stoppage of blood circulation. For the V anchorage, with both straps starting from a single large D-ring, I use a canvas patch of the same goods as the pack, sewed to it with double seams all around the edge, and with cross seams running down from each edge of the D-ring. This multitude of seams makes it proof against being pulled out by a backward tear. There is never any danger from the weight of the pack itself, because that strain comes down the whole seam. For a 2-inch D-ring, a triangular patch of doubled canvas eight inches wide by five inches deep, with the neck slipped through the ring, has proved strong enough for durable service. For a yoke I make one, straps and all, of the same canvas as the pack, ten inches wide by four inches deep where it sews across the back of the pack. The curve of the yoke is a half-circle on a three-inch radius or six-inch diameter, widening in a long slant until, at the lower ends where the buckle comes, the strap is but an inch wide. The strap part is made by simply turning under the edges of the goods one-half inch on each side and sewing the two faces with a seam down each edge and two or three down the middle. This is a strong strap. Its principal trouble is that canvas will not hold eyelets well, so that the buckle tongue sooner or later breaks them out. I prefer sewing with buttonhole stitch wherever, on adjustment, the straps show to need a buckle hole. To fasten the yoke to the pack it needs two seams run all around the edge and two diagonals across the corners. A rivet put in at the two upper corners will prevent the seam starting if it is to be used for very heavy loads. For an ordinary forty-pound load the above scheme is plenty secure enough with twenty cotton thread.

For straps we have the choice of leather or army webbing. I find that the pairs of cartridge yoke straps sold at the army goods stores for 50 cents a pair make good packsack straps. They are used to support the heavy army cartridge carrier, and run over the shoulders like a pair of suspenders, with hooks at the lower ends and adjustable buckles. They are made of wide-woven olive drab webbing, fining down to narrow at the ends. Cutting off one end of each and taking off the metal retaining collar which holds each pair together, I rivet them around the pack D-ring with two tubular rivets. The cut off ends are put on the pack to engage the hooks of the other ends of the straps, taking the place of buckles. The adjustable sliding buckle does the rest in fitting the pack to one's personal measurements.

Many of us are far from any army-goods supply store, but we can all get leather straps. I prefer the 1¼-inch strap of fine strong leather and provide it with a pair of sliders of thick leather 8 inches long by 2½ inches wide. A slit is cut about an inch from top and bottom of these pieces, and they are then slipped on the strap. To use the buckle at the end of each strap you can either cut it off with two inches of the strap fastened to it and then sew these pieces to the bottom of the pack with the hand sewing awl, or else cut the buckle loose entirely and mount it in a canvas anchorage of its own, sewed to the pack canvas on the machine. Very little strain comes on these buckles. They should go well out toward the lower outer edges of the pack; the lower the flatter the pack will hang. Do not try to rivet on leather straps to the canvas. The rivets will surely pull out, tearing a seam in the canvas in doing so, or maybe taking a strip of the canvas with them.

For packsacks, duffle bags, and such camp gear I do not think you can beat ten-ounce waterproof paraffined duck canvas. All the yachting-goods stores and camp outfitters carry it in stock in 29-

and 37-inch widths. It is waterproof, so you are protected against driving spray in a canoe, rain, and upsets. It is strong, easily sewed on the home machine, holds grommets well, does not get smeary in the heat of the sun or stiff in icy weather. I have tried it in all climates and weathers and prefer it to any lighter but less dependable stuff. It comes dyed a dark brown, a good color for all camp gear. Of it I make packs, side-opening duffle bags, pails, anything wanted strong and waterproof. For lighter stuff, such as cook kit, grate and baker covers, I use a light brown strong drilling. For food bags of all sizes, paraffined muslin, which you can buy from the outfitters or make yourself by immersing the goods in a solution of paraffin bricks, shaved fine, turpentine, and a little beeswax. One friend makes a very good solution by dissolving them in gasoline, setting the solution away for a considerable time for the slow process of dissolving to take place.

In sewing up the goods the edge-to-edge outside seam is the neatest, covered with a turn of brown tape. It is no trick at all. The tape is started folded over the seam and held with a few pins. As the work feeds under the machine foot you fold the tape double over the edge of the seam, making sure that both top and bottom are being taken in by the needle. For turning in a hem you just fold over the heavy brown canvas and crease it. Its body of paraffin will make it lie flat, tight down, until held there by the thread.

I give here two designs of packsacks, the square and the army type. The working drawings of the patterns will be all anyone needs to make up one. A brief description of the merits of various pack designs will not be amiss, however. I give you first the Duluth pack, from the home of the pack country, northern Minnesota. A good large size would be the 29 inches by 28 inches by 6 inches, made of ten-ounce brown paraffined duck canvas. Front, bottom, back, and flap is in one long strip, 96 inches long. Cut out two 28-inch by 6-inch sides and sew to strip with outside seam covered with a doubling of brown tape. You have then, roughly, a canvas box of the pack dimensions. Before sewing up it should have been hemmed along top and bottom edges and the D-ring and buckle anchorages sewed on. For a wide pack like this I would prefer two carrying strap D-ring anchorages, spaced about six inches apart. Facing to the rear on the bottom are the two carrying strap buckles, and facing to the front the three flap buckles for ½-inch straps. The tails of these are next sewed on the hem of the flap, and the pack is done. For a smaller 20-inch by 20-inch by 4-inch pack I would use the single large D-ring in the center of the back and lead out my shoulder straps diagonally.

The second pack shown is a modification of the army regulation, and is a type of the long, cylindrical pack that sits low and takes some support from the hips. It is made of a single sheet of 37-inch brown waterproof duck, 56 inches long. It is cut out, as shown in the drawing, to leave flaps 15 inches wide by 10 inches deep at the bottom and 16 inches at top. The edges are then finished all around with doubled tape, and the pack is ready

SIDE-OPENING DUFFLE BAG

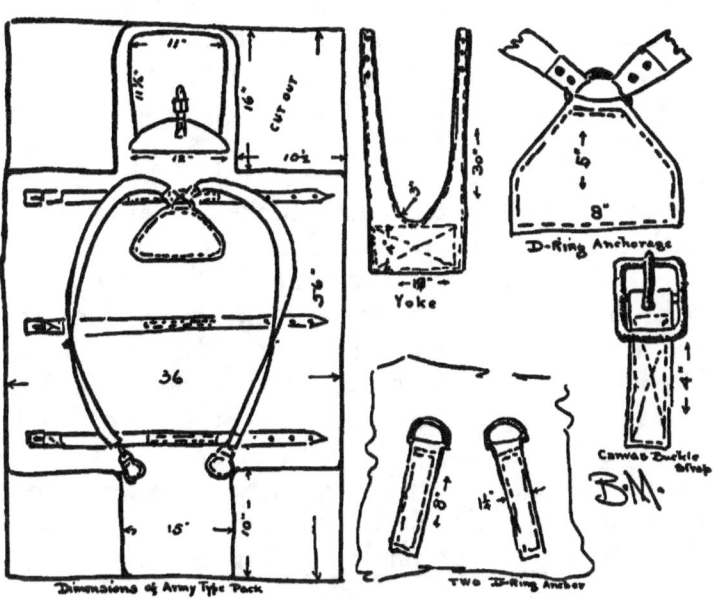

DESIGN FOR ARMY TYPE PACK

47

for carrying and tying straps. The latter are plain ¾-inch by 36-inch leather straps, sewed for six inches in the middle to the back of the pack. They are three in number, the top and bottom ones two inches from the edges of the wide part of the pack and the other one central. Any form of carrying strap that you prefer can next be secured on the back. For a narrow pack like this I would prefer a large two-inch D-ring anchorage at the top and two buckle anchorages sewed to the lower corners just above the lower flap.

On the upper flap is next sewn a bellows pocket with flap, 12 inches by 12 inches being about right. This may be of lighter canvas, but I prefer the same husky waterproof brown duck, as it is to hold grub and will be the thing on your pack most exposed to rain. Two D-rings to secure this mess kit bag are also sewn to the rear edge of this pocket. The pack is now done. To use, you roll up tent, blankets, canned things, etc., to make a long, cylindrical roll about 30 inches long by 10 inches in diameter. Lay this in the center of your pack, fold the cloth around it with bottom flap tucked in, and secure with the three tie straps. The food pocket is then filled with your paraffined muslin food bags, dry poke of socks, night toque, etc., and folded over the top of the pack, where two thongs from its D-rings secure it to the upper tie strap. Needless to say, this is a summer pack. Still, with a light sleeping bag of one-inch quilting, one could tote a winter outfit for short hikes, putting the tent above the quilt bag. The pack itself makes a fair ground cloth to lay under one's bedding on the browse,

being 56 inches long, 16 inches wide at head and
foot, and 36 inches wide where one's body comes.

A third pack that will bear description is the
little rucksack, for short hikes of a few days' dura-
tion. This bag is made of tight-woven waterproofed brown or green canvas of about four-ounce
weight. It consists essentially of a square bag
16 inches high by 18 inches wide, thus requiring a
piece of canvas 32 by 18 inches to begin with.
This is hemmed top and bottom and then sewed
with inside seam; that is, sewed edge to edge and
turned inside out. This is of course the last operation in practical making, for the strap anchorages,
pockets, and upper flap go on first. The strap anchorage is a mere triangle of canvas sewed to the
top, with the 1¼-inch webbing strap slipped under
it to come out in a 45-degree V and secured with
several seams driven through the triangle and
webbing and pack canvas. This webbing goes to
two D-rings at the lower corners of the bag, and is
adjustable by a "suspender adjuster" sliding flat
ring, which can be purchased to fit the strap at a
harness shop. On the front of the pack is sewed a
bellows pocket 7 by 7 inches, with flap, and centrally located at the top rear edge is a closing flap
6 inches by 6½ inches, oval in shape, and finished all
around the edge with doubled tape. A row of grommets is put in all around the top hem after the pack
is sewed up. They begin at the two lower corners
of the flap, and then are spaced three and two inches
alternately around the hem. A cotton rope is
roved through them and secured by a knot beyond
each grommet hole in the upper flap, so that the

rope cannot get out of place or get lost. After filling the bag, this rope is pulled taut, when the bag closes up until its upper edges nearly meet. The flap is then pulled down over it and secured. In the manufactured article this is done for both pocket flap and pack flap by a snap button, but a woodsman would prefer a regular button with buttonhole, as holding more securely, no matter how tight the pack is filled. The snap button has a way of coming undone of its own accord in going through scraggs that will call out many a curse from the bedeviled outdoorsman who may have lost something irreplaceable out of his pack thereby.

This little rucksack will hold an astonishing lot , of plunder. Putting the grub, ammunition, extra clothes, dry poke, and a tent tarp into it, I will roll up my sleeping bag atop of it and go anywhere, in reasonably mild weather, with it. It weighs about twelve ounces.

We now come to duffle bags—easy to make, one of the best rigs for a canoe or hunting trip yet devised. Two of them carried side by side in a leather harness ought to take all the outfit any man should be allowed, and they simply cannot get sunk in an upset nor drowned in a heavy rain storm. The plain 8-inch by 29-inch duffle bag is made by cutting a 27-inch length from your roll of 29-inch brown duck paraffined ten-ounce, hemming the upper end, sewing an edge-to-edge double seam, and turning the thing inside out, when the seam will come inside. A nine-inch circle is next cut and sewn into one end, with a finish of turned-over tape, and a row of grommets is put in the upper end, with a pucker rope to tie it in. If you want a neck, sew in a length of brown drilling before making up the bag, and if a handle in the center side appeals to you, get one out of your brown canvas goods and sew the handle ends to your bag while the canvas is still out flat.

A long duffle bag, end-opening, does not appeal to me much, for the reason that so much has to be pulled out of it and dropped in the leaves (where it seeks a hiding place) before the thing you want can be found. The side-opening bag is more elaborate, but is a winner for general camping or for carrying the grub for a large party. To make it, first of all, a piece of your brown paraffined duck 22 inches long is cut from the 37-inch width of goods. Next, two circles 8½ inches in diameter for the ends, and finally two pieces of brown drilling 8 inches by twelve inches will be wanted for end fillers. These various pieces will sew up to make a side-opening bag 8½ inches by 22 inches long. The handiest places to put the carrying handles will be on the ends, for you will always be pulling those bags out of the bottom of the canoe, and there's a handy place to grab! Make those end straps of brown canvas 6½ inches by 1½ inches, and sew them to the ends, reinforcing with a bit of leather and two rivets.

Inside the bag will be one of its chief conveniences, rows of pockets to hold spoons, forks, salt shakers, and such small deer, or personal belongings if you are using the bag to carry your main outfit. This pocket material is of brown drilling, sewn in in ten-inch loops in three seams about seven inches apart, and the cloth is nine inches deep, although the seam at the bottom is only eight. This leaves the three pockets loose and baggy, so they will hold a good deal. Three more pockets are run, overlapping the upper row three inches, so you have six pockets in which to stow things.

Now as this bag is to be carried by a couple of straps passing around it through a strap handle, it needs two short pieces of leather sewed on the bottom where the straps will pass through. After doing this the bag is ready to assemble. The two lips are first hemmed with a broad 1½-inch hem, and then the round ends sewn in with tape finishing, and finally the drill end fillers are sewn in along the bag edges and the top half of the circular ends, cutting out a half-circle in the goods to match. When done you have a deep side-opening bag with circular ends and bottom. A stick is next slipped into the hem above the inside pockets and two grommets are put in at the ends of both lips. To close, fill the bag with eight-inch friction-top cans of butter, pork, bacon, etc., eight-inch paraffined muslin food bags, until it is full and its contents form a long, eight-inch cylinder. Then match the lips and roll them together around the stick. Secure with the outside straps, and you have a waterproof side-opening duffle bag, ideal for canoe trips or back-packing. To use in camp, drive in two stakes 20 inches apart and hang the bag up on them by the grommet holes in the lip stick hem. It will then hang open with the rows of pockets up and the contents ready to hand. The cook will appreciate the convenience of that bag when he starts a meal for eight, with the thing hung up handy to his fire.

If using it for hiking, the tent and sleeping bag or blanket roll form the cylindrical center of the pack, and one's small personal duffle occupies the pockets. There is room in one end for grub stores— the lower end if you want it to carry well. I would recommend two of them as a good pack for the hunting "sport," who has most of his truck carried by guides. For a stand-on-your-own-feet hiker it has nothing much to attract, as the thing has little use in camp except to form a wall pocket to hang up your spare duffle in. No pack that I take along can be useless in camp. The army pack you can sleep on as a ground cloth. Best of all the light-trip rigs is Dwight Franklin's webbing carrying harness, with his tent and sleeping bag roll forming the outside of the pack itself. He loses no weight in toting anything that has not a use in camp.

CHAPTER IV

Home-Made Tent Stoves and Cook Kits

I LONG ago became converted to the tent stove. It won its way into my heart by sheer merit and against the prejudices of years of camping out before an open fire. Said fire required an axe to be taken along that weighed more than a stove; it required at least an hour's chopping each day, and that hour when one was tired out from the day's hunt and longed to take one's ease. The campfire was bright, light, and cheerful while it lasted, but all too soon it relapsed into smoky embers. And there was no getting away from the drifts of smoke that *would* waft into the tent and stay there! In windy, rainy, or snowy weather it was an acrid eye-watering nuisance, no less! The matter came to the parting of the ways when my State passed fire laws requiring a license to build an open fire in the woods. There were no restrictions on closed fire, *videlicet* a tent stove; but the license for an open camp fire had to be sought from the fire warden of the township in which I proposed to camp. He made matters altogether too complex and "sivilized" for me, so I set about designing my own tent stoves, for none of the outfitters carried anything that weighed less than ten pounds. That was an impossible weight for a hiker!

It seemed to me an unnecessary weight. A tent stove, in the last analysis, is a shell of sheet iron. Light 28-gauge steel is amply heavy enough. I even had a friend who made a very good stove out of a large tin can. Now the stove and the cook kit seem to me to be the most intimately connected. The one should form the container for the other, and the whole thing should go in a brown drilling bag, so as not to get one's duffle smutty. This much settled on, all I had to do was to wrap sheet iron around my cook kit and I had a stove to carry it in, adding thereby about two pounds to the weight to be carried—less than the weight of even a half axe.

This wrapping business is of course figuratively speaking; in practice the wrapping consisted of a well-made stove in 28-gauge sheet iron that just fitted outside the two pots of my cook kit. Camp meals require two or more utensils boiling something at the same time, to be followed by a quick session with the fry pan, when the whole meal is ready to be served and no time lost. As a boiling utensil I have always been very partial to the four-quart aluminum fireless cooker pot. It comes 7½ inches in diameter by 6½ inches deep, with a cover held on by snap hooks on the sides and provided with a flat lifting handle. Two of them weigh a pound, and will boil mulligan and potatoes or rice of quantity for four hungry men. Inside you can pack a set of plates, deep mixing tins, and the six-inch fry pan with folding handle—a whole cook kit; for if the mixing tins are aluminum they make good bake pans by pouring a batter into one, setting it in the stove hole, putting a shallow tin plate on top, and covering it with a pile of live coals.

I first intended making a single cylindrical stove that would take both pots end to end in it, but the trouble with this is that it has only one hole when set up, and a one-hole stove is a sheer aggravation. You need two holes to cook a meal on. All right; put the pots *side by side*, then, and make an oblong stove to just fit around them, and you will have used no more metal than with the simple cylinder. So this was the form the stove finally took. A sheet of 28-gauge iron was first gotten out, 7 inches wide by 36 inches long. This was bent around the two pots and riveted where the metal overlapped in the middle of one flat side. A top was next made, with edges turned over to fit down on the oblong sheet iron sides and lap three-eighths of an inch, when rivets secured it at 3-inch intervals. In this top was cut two holes 6½ inches in diameter to just fit the two aluminum pots. Between them was a narrow bridge left by the overhang of both pot covers. To prevent this bridge sagging in the heat, I riveted inside a narrow reinforcement, a V-shaped piece of 28-gauge. I also cut out two hole covers 7 inches in diameter and provided with three angle stop pieces riveted underneath to keep the covers centrally located on the holes. I am not in favor of a holeless stove for two reasons: first, because you cannot manage the fire properly without being able to take off the lids; and second, because you often have a fine bed of live coals in the stove which would cook splendidly if only you could get the pot bottoms down to it, which you cannot do with a holeless stove. Anyone who has waited for hours for things to cook on a holeless stove will know what I mean.

This stove had no bottom. In setting it up I get a flat rock, or two of them, and chink up around the bottom edges. If more draft is needed than one can get through the door, remove a chink stone or two and she will draw like a major and all be well. Managing a tent stove so it will not smoke is purely a matter of draughts—letting in air enough when wanted to cause complete combustion and prevent smoke. This you cannot do satisfactorily with a bottomed stove, because you are limited to the door draught, which is often not enough.

I put a 3 by 3-inch door in the rear end with a sliding cover in two metal grooves riveted to the shell, and a chimney flue in the bottom of the front end 2 by 3 inches, with lips arranged to engage the bottom of the chimney pipe. This hole was put in the bottom, not the top, of the stove, because the front pot is sure to blank it off when in its hole. It draws just as well if put in the bottom of the stove.

The chimney itself was two 16-inch lengths of 2½-inch pipe. The bottom section had a 2 by 3-inch hole notched out of its lower side and provided with two strips of metal reinforcing, which allowed the lips projecting from front end hole of the stove to slip in between them and the walls of the pipe. To set up, you put the stove on a flat stone, and then shove down the bottom section of stovepipe over the lips, when it would stand fast upright at the end of the stove. The top section I originally made to telescope inside the bottom, but this was a mistake, for after a few camps the bottom section got dirty and caked inside, and the top section would stick in it abominably. I finally made the top section with a slight draw in its end, so it could be put together like ordinary stove pipe. It might seem that a chimney only 32 inches high would not draw well, but such is by no means the case. If the fire is well managed, so as to keep a column of hot air in the pipe it will draw fine if only 14 inches high.

This stove, pipes and all, weighed two and three-quarter pounds, and went with its pots in place in an oilcloth wrapper which formed my ground cloth under the sleeping bag at night. The two pipes went side by side on top of the stove and proved an excellent place to carry fresh meat in, wrapped in the butcher's paraffined paper. I took it on many hiking trips into the mountains during the hunting season. We set it up in the door of the tent and used it for both cooking and tent warming, besides being free from all fire warden's restrictions. To keep the pot bottoms from coming down on the hot coals I bored two $\frac{9}{32}$-inch holes on each side of the stove three inches down from the top. Through these went long $\frac{1}{4}$-inch bolts on which the pot bottom rested.

Meanwhile I had by no means forgotten the possibilities of a cylindrical tent stove. It takes up less room than the oblong, and is easier set up, besides giving a higher and deeper fire. When the

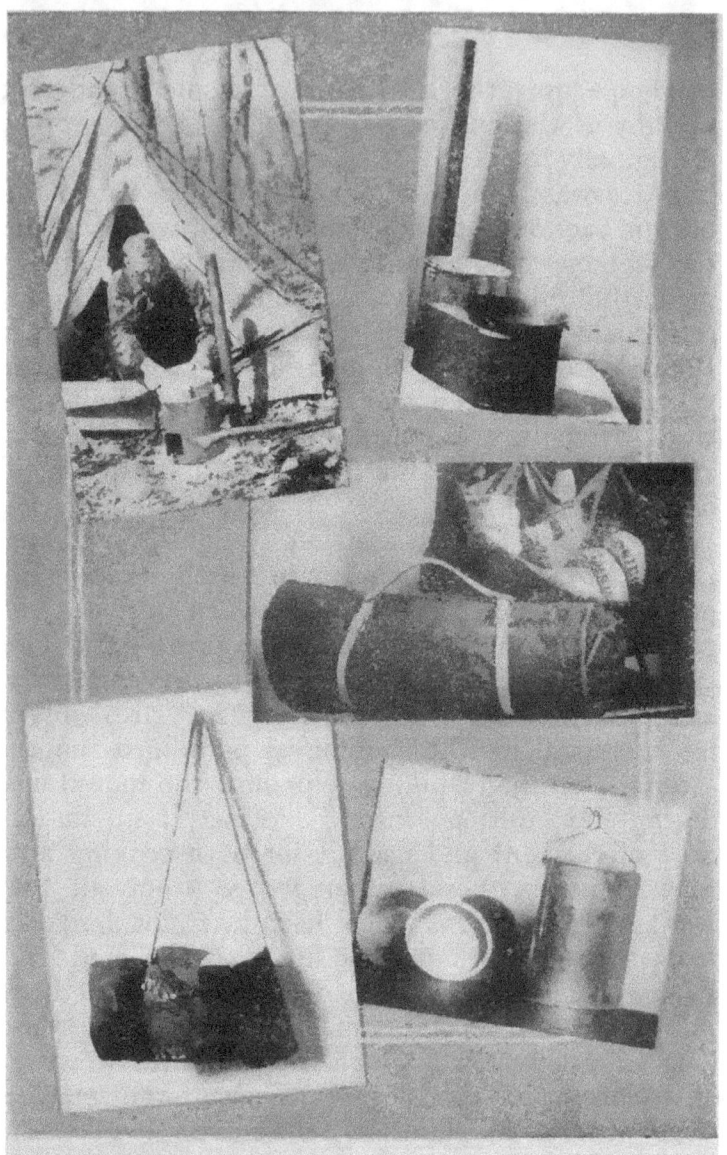

1. 3 Lb. Cylindrical Tent Stove   2. 2¾ Lb. Two-hole Stove
3. Side-opening Food Bags
4. Leather Ditty Bag   5. The Growler Cook Kit

THE AUTHOR'S TWO-HOLE HIKING STOVE

three-section fireless cooker pots came out, all three
forming a circle to go in one hole, I had what I
wanted to make the cylindrical stove a success;
for now you had something that would boil coffee
in one, rice or mulligan in another, and bake a
corn cake in the third. The rather shallow set,
six inches deep, is the one adapted for camp use.
Why? Because the other and deeper set is meant
for a source of heat reaching the walls of the pots
as well as the bottoms, whereas in a camp stove
only the bottoms are reached. The fireless cooker
people intended these shallow sets to go, one above
the other, in the same hole, but we campers had
other uses in mind, for that set would make possible
an ideal tent stove and cook kit for two, to go in a
small closed tent. The set is nine inches in diameter
and six inches deep. Allowing a three-inch coal
bed and an inch of fire space above that, I made
the height of the stove ten inches and rolled up a
steel shell to fit the set snugly. All it then needed
was a three-inch square sliding door in the bottom
front and a circular come-out hole 2½ inches in
diameter cut in the back, with its upper edge four
inches below the top to allow the pots a good
depth. As this stove was to go with my walled
tent, I decided to risk an elbow, so as to have my
stove-hole in the wall instead of the roof of the
tent. Such an elbow, seven inches long over all,
will pack inside the stove. It has a draw at the
stove end so as to drive in snugly into the hole.
A single length of stovepipe 24 inches long by 2½
inches in diameter was made, something that would
lie snug atop my pack. This had a draw to fit into

the elbow looking up, and carried the sparks well away from the roof. This stove weighs two and one-half pounds complete, or four and one-half pounds with the pots in it. There is plenty of room to stow plates, dishes and a nine-inch steel fry pan with folding handle in the lower end. To bake with it I use two deep aluminum plates ten inches in diameter. The batter is poured into one, greased, and the other plate inverted over it. After raising and browning on the bottom, it is capsized and the top browned. Needless to say this is done on the open top of the stove; also that I provided a sheet metal lid for the top when the stove was being used for tent heating.

To do this sheet-metal work one can either make up the stove in cardboard and pin it together, when the whole thing can be taken to a tinsmith and let *him* make it up, or one can do the job himself, *if* he first makes him the indispensable sheet metal folder. The tinsmith has all sorts of conveniences, like rollers, beaders, and crimpers for putting in draws, and he will turn out a workmanlike job. The second stove I had made by a tinsmith for the price of $3.50; and he turned it out with a reinforcing bead along top and bottom edge of the stove, smooth seams, and workmanlike fits throughout. However, with a pair of tinsmith's shears, a folder, drills, and rivets, one can do the job on the home bench. The "folder" is a pair of oak boards with stout hinges, spaced close together so as to withstand the strain of bending sheet metal. Inside the upper board is a rabbet in which is sunk a stout strip of steel, about ⅛-inch metal, say 2 inches wide by 16 inches long. Under the forward edge of it is a shallow rabbet ¼ inch deep. You slip the edge of your sheet in there and fold the upper board over on the lower. It will bend a lip over double on the sheet. Two of these lips in opposite directions form the seam for your pipe or joint. Having no roller machine, you can bend up the pipe over a wooden mandrel with hammer and vise, catch the lip seams and secure by hammering them flat. Riveting jobs are a mere matter of drilling with a breast drill, inserting the ordinary round-head soft steel rivet, and upsetting with a hammer over a piece of iron pipe. By dint of careful hammering it is remarkable what serviceable, if not handsome, tin work can be done at home. My friend, Arthur Stratton, made a splendid reflector baker that way, and I may as well describe it here. The dimensions are given in the drawings. Having gotten out and bent his top, bottom, and back piece all in one strip, he turned over the edges, cut the two sides, and riveted and soldered them together; for Strat wanted to have his baker watertight, so as to use it as a dish-washing container in camp. (By the way, his tent was folded to just fit inside the baker, so he lost no space by it on the trail.) An iron brace of ¾-inch by 18-inch by $\frac{1}{16}$-inch strip iron was next fitted inside the baker, so as to turn in flat against the side when not wanted, and turn up to form a rest for the bake pan when in use. This was riveted through the sides of the baker just loose enough to turn stiffly. Legs were next added, riveted to the sides and provided with a stop rivet to hold them secure when the

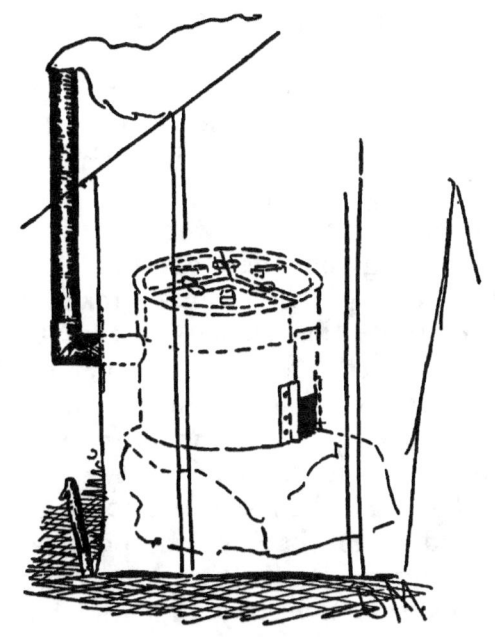

CYLINDRICAL STOVE WITH THREE-PART COOKING POTS

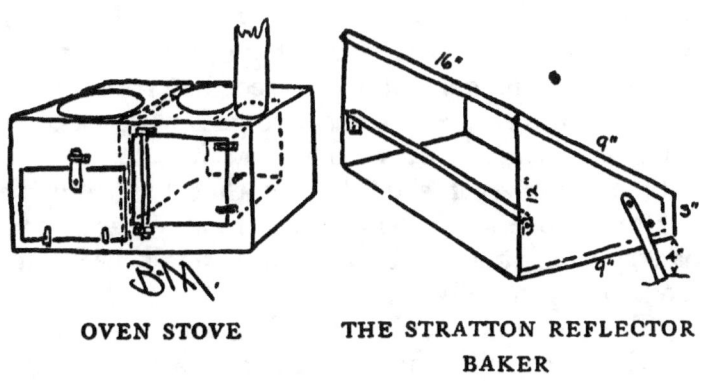

OVEN STOVE

**THE STRATTON REFLECTOR
BAKER**

legs were turned down to rest on the ground, and the baker was done. It worked fine. Many a good mess of corn bread and biscuits have I eaten from it. He had an upper lip on it, so it could be hung over the stove side, when its weight would pull it in snug against the stove wall.

On lone hiking trips I have taken along the little folding grate that came with the Stopple cook kit. It weighs little, folds to 4 inches by 8 inches, and goes in a canvas bag that also holds spoons and forks, so as to keep them and it from getting the rest of the things in the pack dirty. The utensils for the go-light safari consist of a 10-inch aluminum plate, stowed in the back of the pack, an enamel-ware cup hung on the belt with a thong, an oval aluminum baker 9 inches by 7 inches by 1½ inches, with cover, a 6-inch steel fry pan with folding cover, a 6-inch tin mixing pan for cake batters, and a three-quart kidney-shaped tin growler 8 inches wide by 9 inches deep by 2¼ inches thick, with cover. In these arid days I suppose that utensil is no longer manufactured, but it is a whale for small and sudden camps, and goes with me often, slung in a canvas water pail that just fits over it, with a strap over shoulder, so that the thing lies flat under one's left arm. In it I carry fresh meat, packages of bacon, butter, and small perishable foodstuffs generally.

To cook up a meal, the little grate is set up, the growler filled with the elements of a stew or a grab or two of rice in water, the baker unlimbered and set on the grate with a batter in it. The first flare-up of the fire starts off the growler; afterwards a bed of coals is maintained under the grate, so that the cake will not come to grief. After fifteen minutes it is done and set to one side, on edge, to keep hot and the mixing pan goes on the grate to brew coffee or tea. Finally the fry pan is put on to do me a hunk of steak, and when that is done the rice or spuds in the growler report ready, and the meal is served. A light kit. The whole of it does not weigh two pounds.

This grate had two objections: It was not large enough, and its legs were too spindly. It seemed to me that a grate could be devised that would fold up to a mere bundle of rods. So I got me some $\frac{3}{16}$-inch rodding and made a collapsible grate. The two side frames have the legs eyed to them. Across the grate you lay as many rods as seem needful according to the business in hand. The hooks on their ends prevent them from coming off. This grate is 16 inches long by 8 inches wide, and will accommodate a fry pan and a pot at the same time. It weighs a pound. Anvil, vise, pliers, and hammer were all the tools needed to make it.

All wire grates are open to the objection of windy weather blowing most of the heat out from under the pots. A folding three-sided open stove is easily made, 16 inches long by 8 inches wide, with hinges as shown, of 28-gauge sheet metal. A stout bar of iron 1 inch by $\frac{1}{8}$ inch by 16 inches long goes across the open front at the top, and forms a rest for all pots set on the stove. Its two turn-in lips have stud bolts set in them, with wing nuts outside. The ends of these studs project through holes in the top corners of the side, and, clamping up the wing nuts, the stove is ready for use.

From there to a folding camp stove is but a step. It needs a fourth side to engage the two ends with skewer rods, and a cover with two holes and turned-down lip. Dimensions of 8 inches by 8 inches by 16 inches will make a handy little two-hole stove. Door in one end and chimney flue with lips as in the Forester stove to take two lengths of $2\frac{1}{2}$-inch pipe 16 inches long. Back and sides fold up, front is laid on them, and the whole nested in the cover. Put the entire contraption in a flat bag big enough to permit sliding in the pipes side by side, and you have your folding rig. It answers very well where your existing cook kit does not happen to fit any particular stove.

For a hunting party occupying a 10- by 15-foot wall tent, a larger stove than any of these will be needed, something with an oven in it, eight feet of stovepipe, and room enough inside to hold night-logs. As this is packed by horse or canoe, its weight and bulk do not matter. Now, in designing a stove of this character, one decides first on the size of the oven and builds the rest of the stove around that. To take an ordinary 9-inch plate or dish, the oven should be 10 inches deep and the same wide. Eight inches will be enough for the height. Such an oven will go well in a stove 24 inches long by 12 inches wide by 11 inches high, of 20-gauge sheet iron, as giving the right strength for these dimensions. A very good design is shown in the working drawings herewith (page 63). Two 8-inch pot holes are cut in the top, offset as shown, and the flat spaces reinforced underneath with bars of iron 1 inch by $\frac{3}{16}$-inch. Offsetting the holes gives more room for small diametered cooking utensils, like a coffee pot, to find a place while the larger pots set in or on the holes. The oven is located well forward, and the chimney uptake, for four-inch pipe, is in the front forward corner, where it will draw the flames over the oven top. A large filling door is put in the side to add small chips, and the rear end is one large door, on hinges, hanging downward, so that billets can be fed in for night wood while using the stove for tent warming. By opening the side door one can get abundant draft when the fire threatens to smoke for lack of air. This stove will need a bottom to give it strength and rigidity, and is the better for legs, so that it will stand above the forest duff and not start a smoking ground fire in the tent. It weighs about 20 pounds.

The whole art of running a non-smoking tent stove is the judicious use of firewood and drafts. On starting up, the lids should be off and all drafts wide open. A brisk fire is then started, and when giving pure flame the lids are put on, when the flame darts for the chimney as the one available outlet. Once going up the chimney, it heats the walls of its pipe and so establishes a column of hot air which is your draft. Even a short length of pipe kept hot will take off your smoke, the taller, of course, the better, but the principal thing is to have the chimney *hot*. After a bed of live coals is established, add wood as needed, not in big lots which will give off more smoke than the chimney can take care of, but a few sticks at a time. Even then the stove will sometimes start to smoke. The reason is that there is not enough heat going up the chimney, as your hand on it will tell you. Take off a lid, open all drafts, and fan or blow the wood to a flame. When well going, put back the lids and the pipe will draw well, for it now has a heated column of air again established. That is all there is to it.

This article may well conclude with the making of an emergency cook kit. In no big game country should a man set out without a small package of emergency food in pocket or on belt, so that if left out over night he can build a fire, cook a wholesome meal, and make light of the experience. Something to cook in is the first consideration. I find that the square cans that chocolate and cocoa come in make the best emergency tins. It holds about a pint and is 3 inches by 2 inches by 4½ inches high. There is nothing to fit over it manufactured that I know of. Just as it is, with two holes in the lip for a wire bale, it makes a good emergency kit with its cover. I give here a pattern that a friend of mine published for a tin container that would just fit over it, giving him two pails. But as we all carry an enamelware cup hung to our belt, the plain cocoa tin does well enough. A canvas cover should be sewed up for it, with belt straps and a flap. Inside goes the wire bale to hang it over a small campfire with, a package of tea, some lumps of domino sugar, small bags of rice and cornmeal, and a cube of powdered soup. Here also a few bars of emergency chocolate, in case you wish to push on without making any fire at all. Altogether this kit can carry twenty-four hours' rations and weighs a pound.

CHAPTER V
Leather Working

THE leather-working drawer of the sportsman's workshop should have the following tools in it: Hand sewing awl; a set of brass needles, with waxed thread attached, for outside seams; two common awls, straight and curved; a lump of beeswax; a hank of strong linen shoe twine; a keen knife with 45-degree edge for cutting leather strips; a keen paring knife; a sharp two-edged chisel, with $\frac{3}{16}$-inch face for making rawhide seams; buckle-hole punch; eyelet punch and eyelets; tubular rivets, with a blunt cone set punch to set them with; copper washer rivets; screw calk wrench and a box of calks; boot nails and a shoemaker's hammer.

With these in the drawer one is fixed to repair moccasins, fix leather straps and buckles on camp gear, mend moccasins, and make all sorts of leather trail equipment from a ditty bag to an axe scabbard.

A description of the most important tool, the hand sewing awl, may well come first. There are two makes, costing sixty and fifty cents, respectively, at the hardware stores. The principle of both is the same. One has the thread spool mounted in a metal case under the chuck and a set of needles in the handle, and the other has the spool in the handle and the needles in three pockets under the chuck cover. To sew an outside seam with it, the leather edges are matched and set in the vise on your bench. Begin by pulling out about a foot of thread from the spool and threading the end of it through the needle eye, leaving a tail of about an inch. Push the needle through the leather where you propose to begin your seam. Get hold of the thread end and draw all the slack through the hole. Then draw the needle back and punch the second hole of your seam. Pull it back about half an inch, when a loop will push out from the needle end. Shove the end of your slack through this loop, pull the needle out, grab slack and needle in your two hands, and pull tight. The result will be your first lock stitch. You can sew a seam a foot long in ten minutes when you get used to it. When the thread gets used up, add more by pulling back on handle, when a few inches more will come off the bobbin. Needless to say, the length of thread first pulled out should give slack enough to go the full length of the seam on the other side.

The first job that will probably come to this awl will be a moccasin, with half inch or so of the uppers' seam ripped open, as so often happens after a week in the woods. To sew this, you use the bent-point needle and pick out the former awl holes, bending the moccasin so as to throw up the seam handy to get at. For a hole in the toe I find the best scheme is to rip enough of the upper seam to bend the foot "last" down, so you can get at the inner side of the patch seam. For holes in the heel one can get one's fingers down into the moc so as to manipulate the thread slack and feed it through the needle loops. These two holes are the ones that most often afflict moccasins. They are generally *all* that ails them, for the uppers and instep piece are almost always intact. No use throwing away a perfectly good moccasin for a mere hole in the sole! An Indian would not, and he has no sewing awl, either. The patch, of course, goes on outside, where it will not afflict your foot. No less than four pairs of good mocs have gone through my shop so patched—a considerable saving in these days of eight-dollar moccasins!

A knife sheath and a revolver holster are two articles that the enthusiastic camper will often wish to make for himself. All hunting knives come with their sheaths, but the knives get lost and the sheath will rarely fit anything that can be bought in a hardware store. Yet these same hardware-store butcher knives are admittedly the best of camping knives, being of superb steel and very cheap. In making a sheath for one I prefer the overcast rawhide lacing stitch. This can be made in two ways: with a square of the leather showing between each turn of the white rawhide, or with the rawhide in close folds. To make the former the narrow, sharp chisel is brought into play to make slots, and the rawhide worked through as in the ordinary overcast sewing seam. For the latter the chiseled slots are put in at a slight diagonal, so as to nearly overlap each other. When the rawhide is pulled through it meets edge-to-edge, as it will be of ¼-inch strip, which is a trifle wider than the slots cut in the leather. A paper pattern had better first be gotten out for the knife, and then opened out and laid on the leather before cutting out.

The holster is made of stout saddle leather ⅛ of an inch thick. A piece 12½ inches by 10 inches wide will be needed to take a .38 caliber officer's model Colt with 7-inch barrel. The pattern is cut out as shown, 9½ inches from muzzle to top, with cut-out for trigger finger and hanging flap lip projecting up 3 inches. It is then folded over and the edges sewed with overcast rawhide seam. To hang from cartridge belt a loop of the same saddle leather 2½ inches wide by 8 inches long is cut out of the left-over stock, bent double and secured with a flat copper rivet. This is the old-timer gunman rig; allows free movement of the holster when same is strapped to the leg, and is supplemented with a rawhide thong three feet long for securing to leg, rove through two buckle holes in the rear face of the muzzle. I prefer adding to this holster a thong to go over the gun hammer to tie it in when traveling, as I do not want the gun constantly on my mind when going through scraggs, where it is likely to be "frisked" by some passing branch.

A scabbard for the camp axe is another bit of leather goods that the shop is likely to turn out. All belt axes come with their covers on, and only need a bit of seam sewing now and then, but the big axe is more often bought at the hardware store and taken along with its edge tied up in a wad of gunny sacking. This is sure to get lost in a week's camp, and the big axe has a fine time of it cutting things during the trek out to civilization. A scabbard for it will be made of ⅛-inch saddle leather, cut out in one piece with flap, as per pattern. Its

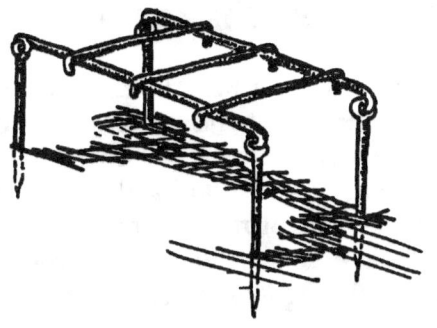

FOLDING WIRE GRATE

**HAND
SEWING
AWL**

WIND-SHIELD GRATE

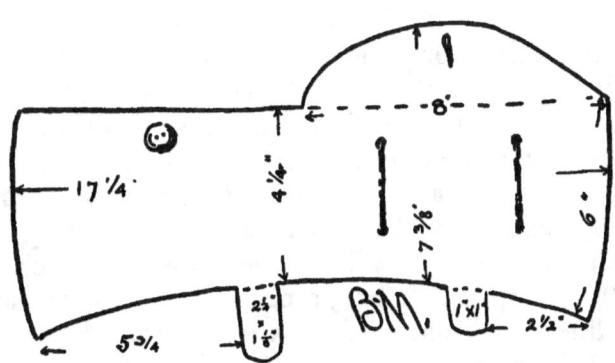

PATTERN FOR AXE SHEATH

73

edges are best fastened with copper rivets, spaced an inch apart, as one cannot depend on a seam to guard the edge. The axe will never go on a belt, yet two slits in the back of the scabbard will not come amiss, for, when lashed atop a horse pack, it helps a lot to feel that a rope is rove *through* those slits, so that the axe cannot get away, although it may come loose.

A mighty useful trail accessory is the ditty bag, that little leather pouch that is carried either by a narrow strap over shoulder or is slipped on the belt by straps for the purpose. It is by no means the unwieldy converted shell bag sold by the outfitters under the name "ditty bag," which they have some-how confounded with the sailor's ditty-box or carry-all. No; the true ditty bag as first described by Ness-muk, the father of modern camping out, is a small pouch about six by eight inches, meant to hold all sorts of small useful things such as easily get lost if carried anywhere in the main pack. Most of these things are heavy. When you want 'em you want 'em bad, but a *very* small pouch will carry all that you should burden yourself with on even a three-weeks' trip into the mountains. Your rifle-cleaning set, your screw calk wrench, set of folding screwdrivers, oil dropper, cartridge extractor, supplementary cart-ridge holder, spare sinkers and fish hooks, screw calks, general utility pocket knife, emergency match safe, a small file, some nails and tacks, a candle stump, a salt box, a can opener, a brass shell case filled with assorted pills and a roll of surgical tape (all in packages, let's hope), a tube of gun grease, some wire, and some chain pot hooks for hanging things over the fire—these are heavy enough for an allowable list.

A good many of my friends and readers who have made up ditty bags on the above dimensions add a bellows side and bottom. This increases the capacity considerably, but I prefer the simple pouch, with flap, sewed up on the sides, with a ½-inch strap going over shoulder, something that will lie flat against one's coat and not tempt the wearer to fill it with so much junk that it becomes a nuisance. Such things as emergency kits, artificial bait lures, etc., belong elsewhere than in the ditty bag. In selecting the strap to carry it, be sure to get a good live piece, not one tanned by chemicals until the leather is doubtful. Then cut it in two and sew the cut ends to the bag, or slip them flat between the side seams and sew all together with the hand awl. The buckle and hole end are then free to adjust, so as to raise the ditty bag well up on the left side, where it will be out of trouble, and the left-over hole end is then trimmed off. Once adjusted, it will not require it again.

One of the best ways to carry a pack is to roll the whole thing—tent, blanket, and a core of small duffle—into a cylindrical pack about 30 inches long by 12 inches in diameter and carry it in a pack harness. The article sold by the outfitters for this purpose does not awaken much enthusiasm. Whoever designed it must have intended it for a cart horse, for the straps are of the heaviest leather, long enough and strong enough to carry a steel safe with. When we reflect that the average sportsman is well content with a forty-pound pack, there

seems little sense in designing a harness to carry
four hundred pounds, which only an Indian can do.
Hence we turn to the shop for relief. Something
light and simple and strong enough for the purpose
is all we wish. I do not like the usual yoke form of
strap for this harness, as it requires a breast strap,
so that the pack cannot be slipped out of quickly
when down in a windfall or in some similar peck of
trouble. Let us try the D-ring, with triangular
canvas anchorage to the upper pack strap, as shown
in the design herewith. This will call for a 2-inch
D-ring, which can be bought from the harness
shop. We will use 1¼-inch straps 42 inches long
for upper and lower pack straps, and get the carrying straps out of good strong leather stock 2½ inches
wide by 18 inches long, tapering to 1¼ inches at
their lower ends. One more store-bought 1¼-inch
strap 54 inches long and an extra buckle for it will
be needed. Of this get out the two carrying straps
that join the upper and lower pack straps, spacing
them side by side and eight inches apart. The
second one will need the spare buckle put on, just
below the lower pack strap, to match the other one,
and the left-over lengths are sewed to the yoke
straps with the hand awl and buckle holes punched
in the blank piece. To assemble this rig, four copper
rivets will be needed, put through at the junctions
of carrying straps and pack straps which go around
the pack. The D-ring yoke is made of doubled
canvas 8 inches wide and 5 inches high, folded
through the D-ring and sewed along the seams and
to the upper pack strap between the two carrying
strap rivets. The wide part of the carrying straps

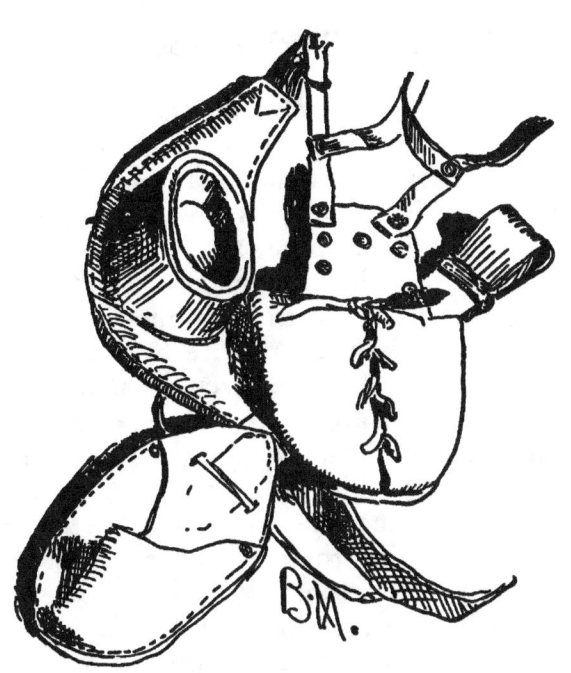

WADING SANDAL AND ROD RESTS

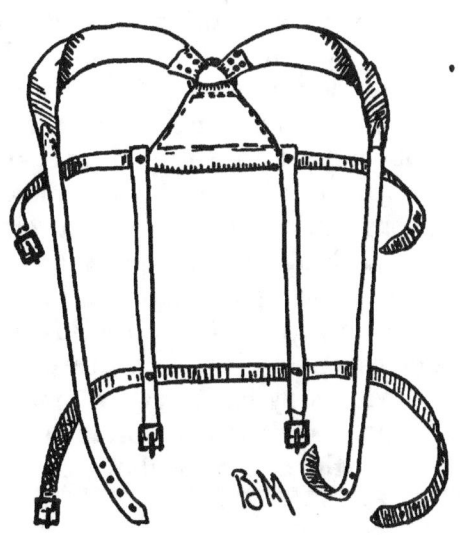

LEATHER PACK HARNESS

77

which go over the big muscles of the neck are riveted through the D-ring with three tubular rivets each. This harness is light, carries well for a cylindrical pack, and is not very expensive to make.

For a heavier load, such as single-tripping it over a carry with, say ninety pounds of duffle on board, you will do better with a tump line, for shoulder straps with this load are sure to compress the chest muscles so as to stop circulation in the arms. The forehead strap of this is a piece of strong, soft leather 18 inches long by 2½ inches wide by ⅛ inch thick, but soft tanned like elk hide. Some makers anchor to it two buckle straps 6 inches long, sewed with three strong seams and provided with a rivet at the lower ends. These buckles allow one to adjust the length from neck to pack to carry it at the right height. I would prefer the anchor strap of 1¼-inch leather, seamed to the forehead strap and fining down to ⅝ inch, where a buckle serves to add on a long six-foot length of shawlstrap ties of ½-inch stuff. Two pairs of the thin strap lengths on a side are enough joined by taking off the buckles, cutting a slit lengthwise near the ends, and slipping one strap through the slit in the other, when they make a close knot which is as strong as the original strap. A little practice in making up the pack will tell within an inch or so of the right length to leave to bring the forehead strap right, when an adjustment of the ⅝-inch buckles on one or both straps gets the length where it will carry easiest. To make up a tump pack, the tent tarp is laid out flat and the tump line laid on it, with its straps about two feet apart. The edges of the tarp are then folded in over the straps, and the duffle piled on them, with the folded blanket or sleeping bag at the bottom, so as to lie flat against back. The tarp is then folded up into a bundle and the ends of the tump lines pulled, shirring the ends of the tarp to close up tight around the duffle. Each strap is then tied and crossed over the pack like tying up a parcel, and the whole thing is cinched up tight and secured. The forehead strap with the 1¼-inch part of the strap will remain in a loop outside the pack. Trying it over the forehead, any further adjustment is made by the buckles and ends of the ½-inch straps where they pass through the buckles.

There are two articles of leather wear in which the fisherman will be mightily interested, and both of which are easy to make in the home shop. The first of these is the leather wading sandal, to strap on over your rubber-boot sole, and so prevent those impromptu sit-downs in midstream which are neither so funny nor so harmless as they look to the streamside observer. The sole of the wading sandal is 8½ inches long by 4 inches wide, fining to 2¾ inches at the instep. It is a tap only, having no heel. Choose good sole leather one-quarter inch thick to make it of. Fifteen hobnails are put in around the edge of the sole, with five more down the center. These are the square quarter-inch wrought-iron hobnails, and the steel points of them are upset over small ⅜-inch copper washers inside the sole.

Over the toe of the sole goes the vamp, of soft, tough ¹⁄₁₆-inch leather. It is made in two pieces, laced down the center with rawhide thong. Each half is a spherical triangle, 4½ inches across the base, 5 inches on the lacing edge, and 6 inches along the seam, which sews along the edge of the sole. The two halves are sewed to the sole by turning in the edge all around and running the seam inside the sandal, which is permitted because the vamp is in two halves, so you can get inside it to run the seam with the hand sewing awl. When done, the leather will naturally curve over to form a wide leather vamp that will fit over the toe of a rubber boot. Four lacing holes are then punched in the edges and a short thong run through them, by which the vamp can be laced snugly over the toe of the boot.

To secure the heel, two ⅝-inch straps are riveted to the two rear corners of the sole inside with copper washer rivets. The buckle strap is 5 inches long, the hole strap 11 inches. This pair is to strap over the instep of your boot. To these two straps are riveted a second pair, 2 inches up from the sole rivets, to go around behind the heel and prevent the sandal coming off backward. The buckle end of this pair is 4½ inches long and the hole end 9 inches. After securing the instep strap this latter pair is buckled around the heel, and the sandal is on to stay.

The second article of leather work I have in mind for fishermen concerns more nearly the salt-water angler, and is the rod rest, without which one is "out of luck" when fighting a determined channel bass of some 30 pounds' weight. There are two forms of this rod rest: the pocket type, hung from the front of one's belt, and the sole-leather socket rest tied loosely around the waist with a strap of its own. The former is the easiest to make and lightest to carry in a pack. It is simply a $\frac{1}{8}$-inch leather back, 4 inches wide by 6½ inches long, with a 1½-inch strap 18 inches long sewed to it at the upper end with a 2½-inch lap for the seam. The front of the pocket is 5 inches wide by 5 inches deep, cut away on its upper edge in a curve that comes down to 3 inches deep in the center. It is sewed to the back with a single seam, so as to bag out in front, due to its extra width, and has two tubular rivets put in at the upper corners to prevent the seam starting. A buckle hole is also punched in the bottom to let water run out if the fisherman gets a douse of surf spray. The long 18-inch strap is doubled over backward and secured, in the manufactured article, by two snap buttons. These require a special tool to set them, and come in boxes of several gross, containing the various parts of the male and female ends, but as this is rather an expensive outfit to purchase, the home shop will be content with a button and a couple of slits for it, cut in the strap so it can be adjusted at the right height. A narrow leather collar is put around the strap, so as to slip up over it and hold it flat and secure to one's belt. To put this rod rest on, you slip the loop through your belt and tighten the collar up against the belt. Two large holes are punched in the back piece on each side of the strap end, and through these holes are rove a strip of rawhide lacing to tie the holder to one's leg. I seldom use this feature myself, as, once the rod butt is in the pocket, it stays there, and I prefer the pocket free to move instead of being strapped fast to the leg.

The socket type of rod rest has the advantage of not making such a drag on your belt, as its strap goes over the hips around your back, so it is far less fatiguing to wear. It is made of two pieces of sole leather 8 inches wide by 4 inches deep, of the shape shown in the drawing. A belt of $\frac{7}{8}$-inch leather is seamed into the ends of this sole-leather back, the buckle end 10 inches long, the hole end 30 inches. This is long enough to go on outside a canvas coat or mackinaw, such as the surf fisherman is often glad to wear on cold autumn nights. The socket for this rest is a collar of sole leather, 3 inches wide by 2½ inches high, 2¼ inches deep at the lower end and ¾ inch deep at the upper end. To make it, the thin ¾-inch ends of the collar are shaved down, so as to overlap about an inch, and then seamed together. The pattern for it is 10½ inches long. When set on the sole leather back piece its lower side sticks out on a bevel of about 30 degrees. When trimmed and shaved to lie flat all around the collar, it is then sewed to the front face of the rod rest with a bevel seam.

To assemble this rod rest, the two flat pieces and the collar are first cut out, the collar bent into an oblong ring and sewed with a seam around its shaved ends, and the collar then fitted to the front piece and sewed to it. The ends of the straps are next set in and the back piece put on, after which a seam is run all around the edges, including two extra V seams to give additional anchorage to the strap ends.

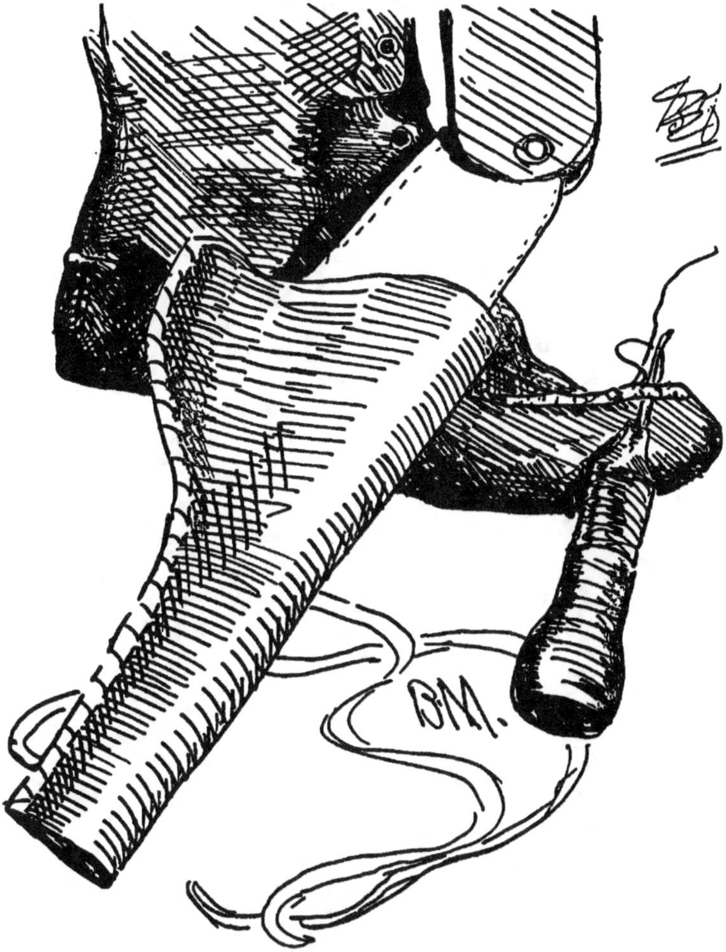

GUNMAN HOLSTER AND MOCCASIN SEWING AWL

RAWHIDE STITCH KNIFE SHEATH

83

CHAPTER VI

Decoy Making

With a Footnote on a Duck Battery

AS I look back over the various shops that I have worked and sung and puttered and burnt pounds of good old tobacco in, the one I love best is my shop of boyhood days. I was a lonely critter; could play no known game (if there were nine boys in the field I played right field; if ten, I was put off the team), and most of my time out of school was spent in the woods, or on the waters, or in my shop. That shop had every known tool in it, and it had a jigsaw. I wish I had a jigsaw now! For if I had I would cut out my own decoys instead of sending the patterns to the mill to be shaped out on a band saw. My boyhood foot-power jigsaw could easily cut out snipe decoys, and, if provided with a husky saw for inch soft timber, could saw things out of that, too. For the best duck decoy is hollow, and the easiest way to make it is to saw out a set of flat sections with the centers cut out via jigsaw, and then screw them up, layer by layer, to make a hollow duck decoy. The back and bottom are solid boards, of white pine, white cedar, or spruce. The three center layers are all cut out inside, so that when screwed up there is a cavity. The decoy will then weigh about 2½ pounds, and will last forever. I give here a set of patterns for the sections, for which I am indebted to Mr. Aldo Leopold, of *Forest and Stream*, who makes his decoys hollow. Anyone can enlarge the patterns on the stock planks and cut out either with a good key-hole saw or the shop jigsaw, or send to the mill and have them done on a band saw. They are assembled, beginning with No. 5, by four to six wood screws, countersunk, and made watertight with a wipe of white lead paste between the plates. The bottom board goes on last, and then a session with chisel, spokeshave, and rasp file is in order. Finish with sandpaper. The heads are gotten out of 2 inches by 4 inches pattern pine stock, the outline being cut out with either chisel and augur bit or key-hole saw. If a quantity of these are to be roughed out this is certainly the job I would send to the mill!

Walter Sawyer, of beloved memory, preferred cork for his decoys, both duck and snipe. His dimensions are: 14½ inches by 7½ inches for black ducks and mallard, and 12½ inches by 6 inches for broadbill and redhead. He bought the rough commercial cork from the New York importing houses, just as it came from Spain overseas. It comes in slabs 1½ inches to 2½ inches thick, uneven and irregular in surface. But an ordinary rasp horseshoe file will work it like cheese. Marking the oval on a 2½-inch slab for black ducks, he would saw it out with a key-hole saw and file both faces to a smooth fit in no time with the rasp. Two slabs, doweled together with maple dowels, which you can buy very cheaply at any hardware store, gave him the rough body, which was then formed to shape with the rasp. The duck head was of white pine, of 1¾-inch stock, dressed. The outline was cut out first with the jigsaw or compass, and then whittled to a neat job.

With both types, hollow wooden and cork, the first thing to do, after fastening on the heads with a dowel run down through the head to come out at the base of the breast, was to set the decoy afloat and put on a trial weight, to find where and how much she would need of ballast to trim her. Around the spot was then chiseled a shallow square, in which a couple of tacks were driven. Turning the decoy bottom up and level, molten lead was poured in. It sets quickly and does not burn the wood. The tack- or nailheads hold it securely in place. A stout screweye or staple or leather loop, in salt-water gunning, was then driven in below the breast for the anchor rope, and the decoy was ready for finishing.

Dull-finish paint, with excess of turpentine and dryer, is what is needed. The plumage of the real duck does not shine, no matter what the angle of the sun, yet how often have we noticed a whole flock of decoys gleaming white as the rising sun strikes their smooth-finished bodies! The fraud is plain to Sir Mallard, who has far keener eyes than you or I, and can see that flash as well as he sees your dark hat in the blind if you are foolish enough to wear one. Shiny finish is, however, admissible in those parts of the duck plumage that are naturally of metallic sheen, such as the head and wing spec-

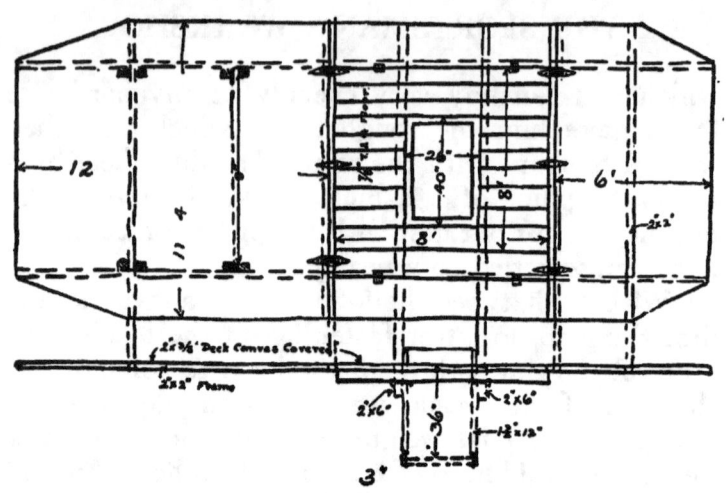

DUCKING BATTERY DESIGN

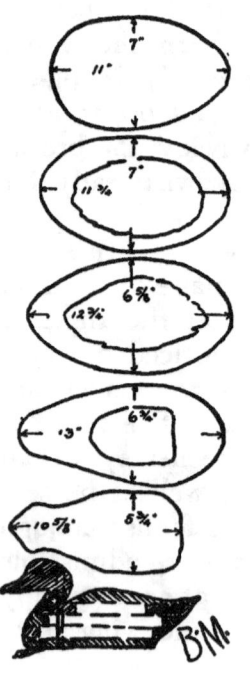

**PATTERNS
FOR
HOLLOW
DUCK
DECOYS**

**DUCK
AND
CROW
STOOLS**

ulum of mallards, and the wing speculum of almost all species.

In coloring up decoys the gunner will select the ducks that abound in his own section. Two sizes of decoys will answer for all species, the mallard and the scaup size, as will be noted from the following table, giving the normal sizes of various kinds in two groups:

Mallard	23″	Greater Scaup	18″
Black Duck	22″	Lesser Scaup	17″
Baldpate	21″	Redhead	18″
Sprig	24″	Teal	15″

For coloration one can copy from any of the thousands of pictures of popular duck species that exist on calendars, magazine covers, etc.

The head should be well cheeked, to full width of pine stock, and bill nicely finished and painted true to natural coloration. Mr. Leopold is very insistent upon altering the position of each head in his flock, a good idea, as contributing to the life-like appearance of the stool, for even a human being notices decoys and tells them from real ducks, principally because all the heads face fixedly straight ahead. You may recall that point yourself when you came to a decision whether a given flock of ducks were decoys or not. I would go him one better, and that is to arrange at least three or four of my decoys to upend so that the tail and part of the body only show above water. Who ever saw a real flock of ducks in which at least one or two were not feeding! To do this in practice, I drive. a small wire staple in the breasts of some of them and bring along some lead weights that have been tested out at home as heavy enough to upend the decoy. These are hung on the ones selected.

The question of eyes is well worth giving careful attention to. One paints the circular iris with a fine brush, but the pupil should be a glass-head tack of the right color. These may be had by a raid on the ten-cent store, where pins of various colored heads may be bought. Cutting the pins to tack length, you have the commodity you need.

A final decoration that Walter used a good deal with his decoys was to tack on real wings. He saved those from many of the ducks shot, kiln-dried them in the oven to cure the meat, and then tacked them to his decoy bodies. Walter always swore by that scheme, and claimed that ducks stooled better to his winged decoys than to any others.

The second large division of decoy making is of shore birds. My boyhood shop turned out quantities of the flat wooden decoys, sawed out of ¾-inch pine stock on the jigsaw. These, when painted up, carried easily and answered very well for the unsuspicious snipe of that far-off period. Nowadays the larger shore birds have become wary and suspicious, and a full-bodied decoy is needed. The folding tin ones are fine, for those who can afford them, carry well in a pack on a beach hike, and have but one disadvantage, and that is that when the surf downs one he is gone beyond recovery. The wooden and cork decoys float, and are either cast up on the next comber or can be retrieved by going in after them. As most snipe shooting begins in the early dusk before dawn and by aid of a duck boat, a couple of dozen solid snipe decoys, either wooden or cork, will generally be found piled in the stern rack.

Standard snipe dimensions are 10½ inches from crown of head to tip of tail, by 3½ inches deep, measured from full of breast to back. This is for black-bellied plover. Lesser yellow-legs, 10¼ inches by 3½ inches; greater, 11½ inches by 3¾ inches; robin snipe and dowitchers, 9 inches by 3 inches; surf snipe, 8 inches by 2½ inches. These measurements do not include bills. For willet and greater yellow-legs the bill should be whittled of locust or pinoak, with a neat taper flaring properly at the head. For the plover a large nail or telegraph wire driven through from the back of the head imitates well enough the thin, bluff bill of this species. Leg sticks 24 inches and 30 inches long should be provided for these decoys, as the short 12-inch leg made by the tin-decoy manufacturers is only useful in the little surf snipe, now all protected by the federal migratory bird laws. As seen from a distance the most noticeable feature of a real flock of feeding shore birds is their *height*. They look like cranes looming up on the strand. A thirty-inch leg is none too long, after shoving down to get a good anchorage in the mud.

Snipe decoys may be sawed from profile out of 2-inch pine stock, or rasped out of cork slabs, of which the left-over pieces from duck decoy making will provide plenty of stock. Our sketches give the markings of five of the most used species of snipe decoys. They should be dull finish painted, with black pin-head eyes.

The principal art in snipe shooting is to learn the whistles of the different kinds, and how to distinguish them at sight when flying in a flock far over the green marsh horizons. The usual tendency to whistle the yellow-leg call for any and all snipe seen is stupid to a degree. If the flock happens to be black-bellies or curlew they will have little inclination to respond to a tattler call. As the human whistle has but a short range, you will find that most of the baymen have a bone whistle that they swear by, generally home-made. It has the wild twang that is absent from the human whistle, and, once having made a bone one, with the proper pitch and tone quality, your bayman would not part with it for several farms! A thin leg bone, about 3 inches long by ½ inch in diameter is good stock to work on. Cut a lip and mouthpiece in one end, and whittle for it a wooden whistle plug. Blowing on it, you get the lowest note of the call, shortening the other end with the hacksaw until just right. The second note is got by boring an eighth-inch hole about ¾ inch from the end. A second one goes in ½ inch further up the shank from that, and you have the *hu-hu-hu!* of the yellow-leg. There is still room for a third hole, about an inch below the lip, which will give the high note of the two-note call of the black-bellied plover. Closing all but that one, you open the second hole down, and get the *wee-you!* of the black-belly. A trial whistle will give some idea of just where the holes should go to give the exact pitch. The shape of the bone, well scraped out inside, gives the snipy timbre so much desired.

And, while making decoys, do not overlook a crow stool, 14 inches by 4 inches, whittled out of two slabs of 2-inch stock and doweled together. The crow is a large bird and wary; anything undersized will keep him at a safe distance. During the closed season, with a .22 rifle and a hide near said decoy, stood out in a field, one can have plenty of sport and do the farmer a service while getting good practice the while.

I promised a footnote to this chapter on building a battery box. There is no published drawing of this that one can work to, except a plan view that has become incorporated in a handbook compiled by the writer some time ago. The central feature of this battery is a sink box, 40 inches by 26 inches by 36 inches deep, set crosswise in the raft so that two gunners can squat in it side by side. It is built of heavy 1¾-inch pine stock, dressed, and is caulked in the seams and painted outside. The battery is 26 feet 6 inches long by 11 feet 4 inches wide. A stout platform 8 feet by 8 feet is first built around the sink box on 2 inches by 6 inches beams, bolted to the 40-inch edges of the box. This platform is then laid down in ⅞-inch tongue-and-groove stock. A forward frame 12 feet long by 11 feet 4 inches wide is then gotten out of light 4-inch by 1¼-inch stock and decked over with 2-inch strips, canvas covered. This is not to be walked on, but serves to steady the raft from tipping and keeps the waves off. It is hinged to the raft in the bayman's outfit, or it may be carried separately and bolted to it when the battery is assembled. Astern of the raft goes a similar float, 6 feet long by 11

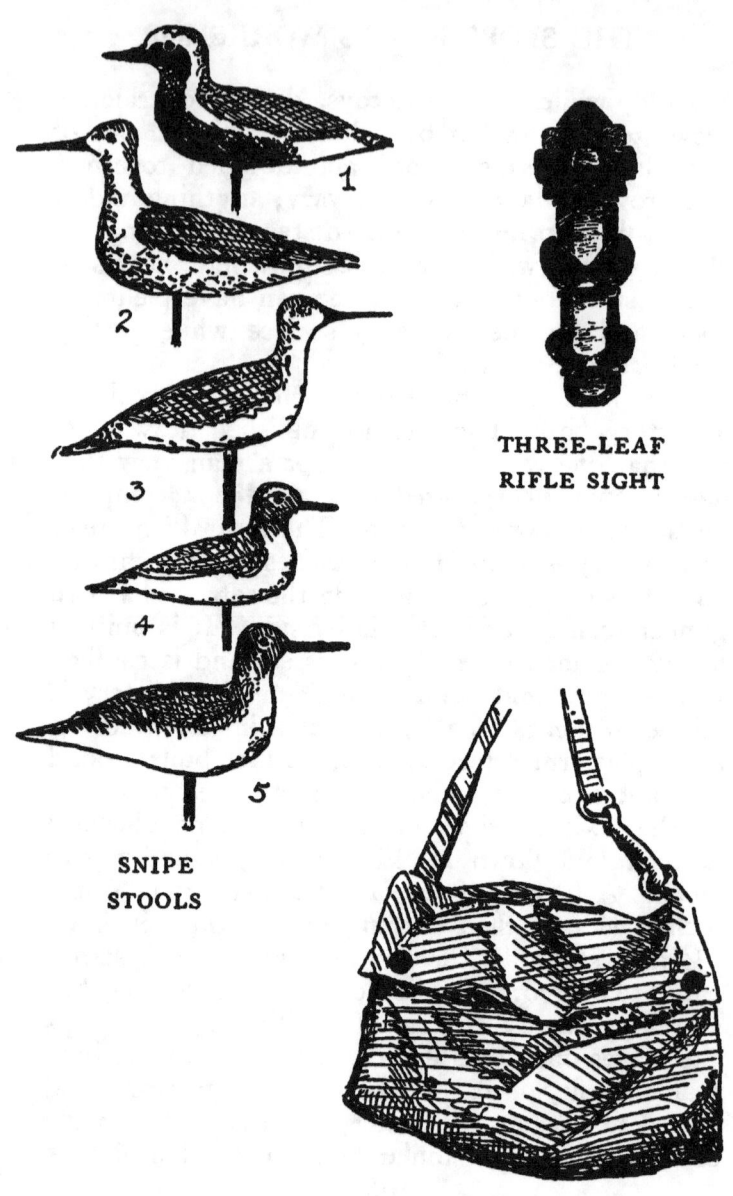

THREE-LEAF
RIFLE SIGHT

SNIPE
STOOLS

LEATHER DITTY-BAG

93

feet 4 inches wide, made the same way, bolted or hinged to the rear edge of the raft. Two narrow strips of the same material are let in, 8 feet long by 20 inches wide, to fill out the sides between the front and rear floats, and the battery is assembled. The whole raft lies flush with the water, the movable end and side floats taking the swell of the waves and preventing a wash coming inboard. Around the lips of the box are lead flanges which can be turned up four inches to prevent a thin wash, sweeping over the battery surface, from lapping into the sink box. Let into the plank floor of the raft are two long boxes, a foot wide by six feet long, in which are put the iron weights that sink the box down to water level after the men have gotten in and one can tell how much more weight is necessary. About two hundred pounds will be needed.

CHAPTER VII

The Gun Shop

UPON the gun bench of the sportsman's workshop falls the upkeep and repairs of his arsenal, and, if he is one of those delightful souls who love to putter, the reloading of his shotgun and rifle cartridges. The old-timer can read the character of any sportsman by a single glance at his gun cabinet, a single inquiring look through the barrels of his iron-mongery. It is a fact never sufficiently taken to heart that a very little rust and corrosion does more to ruin the shooting qualities of a good barrel than a thousand shots fired from it. Look through your friend's gun-barrels—or, let us say, your own—if they show rust and worse, he, she, or *you* may be convicted at once of laziness, carelessness, and that happy-go-lucky spirit that hopes for the best and charges all failures up to "luck." But if the guns are spotless inside and out, and a nice coating of good gun oil shines in the bore, you can lay to it that that owner is a good man to camp with, careful, thoughtful of the well-being of the faithful shooting irons that will mean so much to him when the big moment of the next trip comes, and possessed of a quiet pride in the efficiency of the tools he works with that stamps the real woodsman.

And so your gun drawer will be well equipped with shotgun- and rifle-cleaning implements, ammonia solution for removing metal fouling, rust removers, nitro solvents, and gun oils. In addition, we will look for the right files and screwdrivers, crocus cloth, lead plates to put in the vise jaws, so as to hold guns without marring the metal finish, and a few small clamps to compress lock springs. Also a brass mallet and a couple of hardwood billies for driving out this and that, and at least one long-nosed, hard steel punch for starting pins.

The shotgun arsenal will not require much attention if well cleaned and oiled after each day afield. Occasionally the safety in some makes gets gummed fast by salt wrack getting into the locks; but aside from this it is seldom that Sir Shotgun requires anything but cleaning. It is rather different with the rifle. As it comes from the factory, it is every man's weapon, with no carrying strap, no checking on fore end or tang, and the cheapest set of sights that can be described as reasonably efficient. Now a rifle is such an intimate part of the hunter as to require a good deal of adaptation to the particular eye and arm and trigger finger of its owner. The sights will do fairly well "as is," but much finer shooting can be had by changing them to ones more adapted to your own tastes and eyesight. You owe it to yourself to equip your rifle with the front, rear, and tang peep sight that you have found you shoot best with. The rear leaf sight should have facilities for instantly changing the range, with 100 yards as its zero, while the rear tang peep is to be set and left at 100 yards. For general shooting at this range the tang peep is the most satisfactory, because of its clear vision of the game and the front sight; but in dim lights or uncertain ranges you will want the rear sight only, so that you can cut off as much or little of the front sight as judgment tells is right, or can throw up the two hundred or three hundred yard bar at will. It goes without saying that the rear sight should lie flat on the barrel if the peep is being used. Nothing is more confusing than *three* sights, the rear one cutting off, as usual, part of the front.

My own personal preferences are for a plain steel front sight, silvered over the rib. This is strong and reliable. Too often have I gone into the woods with companions who found their expensive ivory bead front sights knocked off before even the rifle had left its case, and we had to hammer a new blade out of a lead sinker, fit it to the rifle, and sight her in the camp. No; the good old all-steel front sight *suits*, and the way to make it equal any bead is to just file a little forty-five-degree flat on its upper rear face. This makes a little looking glass, say a sixteenth inch high by the width of the knife, a tiny white mirror that will reflect the sky light back into your eye earlier in the morning and later in the evening than any bead, and it will not "shoot off the light" as the bead does; that is, show a bright point on the side of the bead where the sun reflection comes, thus making the shooter take that side as the center of his bead. Never yet have I had trouble with this front sight. It sticks up like a white bar over the rear sight, visible in all lights, and all white in the sun glare. I have had military leaf sights get loose on their pins, making me shoot "all over the lot;" have had ivory beads crumble on an unsympathetic granite boulder, and gold beads turn up missing, with no explanations except that I must have knocked it off somewhere during the day's climb; but never yet has the old steel front failed to be there. In fact, for the last ten years I have never given it a thought!

The rear sight should fold flat on the barrel. Mine has two leafs, a deep-notch wide V, which I seldom use except for very fine still sights; and a flat bar with ivory triangle, point up, showing the center of the bar. This I use for all woods shooting when it is too dim for the peep to define well. I would prefer a three-leaf sight, three bars with the same triangle in each, giving me one, two, and three hundred yards with a push of the thumb. Before going on a Rocky Mountain hunt for goat and sheep I certainly would buy one and put it on. The present sight, set for 100 yards, will do for Eastern shooting.

To put in a new sight is the simplest thing in the world. The dovetail on the barrel draws from right to left. Knock out the old sight with mallet and a short piece of brass rodding. Put in the new sight until it begins to draw hard. Then bore-sight the rifle; that is, set it up firmly bearing on a distant mark, which you can see looking through the bore, and then drive the rear sight in until it and the front also line up on the mark. As this cannot be done with a lever action rifle, the procedure in that case will be to scratch a center line on the barrel dovetail from the old sight center, and drive in the new until it coincides. It is then roughly sighted; but to get it right for the rifle's zero take out a target and shoot groups on it, moving the rear sight until they center around the bull's-eye.

Suppose, however, they shoot high? someone asks. That will mean that you must watch to see just how much of the front to cut off with the bar to shoot true center. Remember how much it was and carry it always in your mind's eye, for it is the rifle's range zero at one hundred yards. Of course if you are sighting in at a fifty-yard target the groups will come high anyhow, and the published mid-range trajectory of your cartridge will tell you how much high to expect the groups. If the rifle shoots low, with a coarse sight showing, file off some of the knife until you get a fair amount over the bar for a hundred yards.

The next sight improvement for the shop to make is to put on a peep. For a light rifle a receiver peep is all right, for one can bend the head forward to get one's eye close to it; but for heavy rifles of big recoil I prefer the tang peep, as the receiver peep is almost useless in dim light. For a rifle like the .32-20 the receiver peep is very handy, however. It comes with its pivot screw attached, and the hole for it is already bored and tapped in the receiver frame. Back out the dummy screw in that hole and put in the receiver peep frame. It has a cam lever on it, by which the peep can be instantly raised to 200 and 300 yards and fractions thereof. If you want to use your rear open sight, the cam can be loosened and the whole receiver frame raised so you can see under it. The old buckhorn notched sight should be taken off and a folding leaf sight put on, for the buckhorn is very much in the way; in fact, a hindrance if using the peep.

In selecting a tang peep for your big-game rifle the first thing to be considered is the recoil. The receiver frame will kick back about 2½ inches with good hard holding, so that about 3 inches from the eye is the limit distance to set the tang peep back toward your eye. The tang peep sold for the Model '95 Winchester sets it so far back as to land right into the eye in prone firing, and to bark the eye socket painfully with off-hand and kneeling positions. It was evidently designed to clear the bolt, with no thought whatever of the shooter's optic. However, the remedy is a Model '94 sight, which sets nearly ¾ inch further forward on the tang. It should be spring-folding, so as to fall back when the bolt rides over it, and then return to shooting position when the action is closed. This sight is the one I put on my .35 Winchester, and has given entire satisfaction. It comes mounted on a flat steel bar, with screws and holes to fit one's already bored and tapped in the upper tongue of the receiver frame. There is a setting wedge, by which it can be held fast when laid back on the tang and not wanted, and the shank of the peep is graduated in fifty-yard marks, with a knurled sleeve to raise or lower it quickly, and a knurled outer sleeve to lock the other one fast. After putting it on, it needs throwing to right or left to bring the peep in exact center, and this is best done by loosening the tang screws and inserting a thin strip of visiting card under one edge, until the peep shoots zero with the rear sight, when the screws are tightened up on the cardboard as tight as they will go.

The next thing your rifle will need is checking the fore end and tang grip. It is impossible to get a good sight with sweaty fingers on smooth oiled walnut, and in big-game hunting you often are forced to shoot in just that condition, breathless from a furious run or climb, and sweating like a bull. Checking a good grip is not so hard as it looks, and is more than worth your time. The nicest way is to buy a checking tool from any of the big gun stores. This tool parallels its own lines which is always the great trouble with home-shop checking jobs. The first one I tried I worked out with a pencil design, scribing with a sharp tool, deepening the scores by working over them again and again, and finally finishing with a knife-edge file. It made a good grip, but not very pretty to look at, because the lines *would* not come exactly parallel by reason of the drag of the grain of the wood on the tool. The regular checking tool cuts one line while scoring the next. It costs perhaps seventy-five cents at present prices, but it is the thing to use. For a fore-end design I prefer a long diamond over the lower center, with a half diamond meeting it on each side, the long upper line of the half diamond running $3/8$ inch below the upper edge of the fore end. The tang design should be a long sweep, beginning just below the tang peep base, and running back in a slant to a center under the stock, $2\frac{1}{2}$ inches back of the lever end. Run the bottom outline $1/4$ inch around the lower frame tongue and the same around the top tongue, carrying it down ¼ inch back of the receiver frame butt. This outline is filled in with checking, and makes a good right-hand grip. Checking is not all ornament, let me tell you! It has its very definite use in the art of shooting.

The next shop job on the rifle will be putting on the strap. For all western shooting, where there is plentiful mountain climbing, and both hands and both feet may be needed for it, a strap is a necessity, and I, for one, want a strap in the East, too. Some use the military strap, which is long enough to wind around the arm and aid in steady holding. Out of the question, of course, in big game shooting, being too slow; but my own strap does all that instantly, and is also the right length for carrying over shoulder or on the back when climbing. This length is so adjusted that when the rifle is at shoulder and the crook of the left elbow is slipped inside the strap a powerful triangle of forces is at once set up which steadies the rifle like a rock against right shoulder and left hand fore-end grip. And this is instantaneous, too, done in the act of raising the rifle to aim. The right strap length (for me) to do this is 2 feet 4 inches; one alters this length for one's personal measurements until the rifle comes up and locks fast in your holding just right. To put on the strap you need two flat bronze strap rings, which can be bought from any big gun store, the stock ring hinged and put on 3½ inches from the heel, and the fore-end ring swiveled and put on with a plate inside the fore-end, 2 inches back of its knob. The strap itself is of soft ⅛-inch leather,

**FOLDING
LEAF
SIGHT**

BULLET MOULD

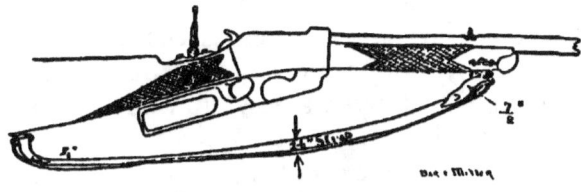

**RIFLE
CHECKING
AND
STRAP**

**THE
CLEANING
BRUSH
FOR THE
TRIP**

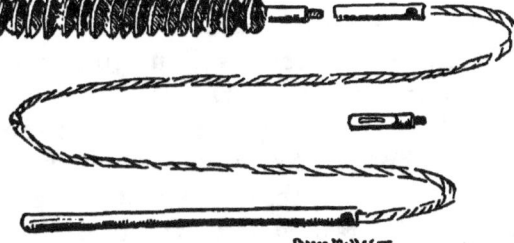

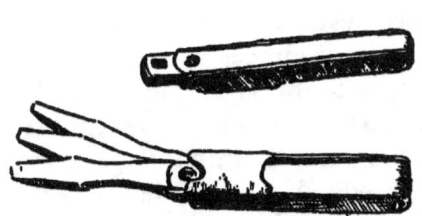

RIFLE SCREWDRIVERS

FLEXIBLE PEEP

1¼ inches wide, fining down to ⅛ inch, where it passes through the rings. The strap is 3 feet long altogether, and is adjusted by two bronze buttons, very like the ordinary collar buttons, which pass through slits in the leather, securing the two ends of the strap doubled under the button. This is a very much better arrangement than a buckle with buckle holes, which would always be catching in scraggs and digging one's hands with its tongue. The fore-end ring should be swiveled, so as to let the strap lead out flat across the shoulder at all angles of twist. This pair of buckles cost $1.00, if I remember correctly, but were well worth it. They have been on the rifle six years now, and never have given the least trouble.

As I said before, it cannot be too much emphasized that the most important thing about a rifle is to keep it clean. Modern smokeless powders are extremely corrosive, and form a wash or plating of copper and acid salts that will ruin the barrel if left there. Gun grease and rust remover will not take it out. The only thing to use is strong ammonia. If you think your rifle is clean, after swabbing and scraping with the brass brush until a rag comes out clean, just run in one soaked in ammonia and watch the black residue pour out! Colonel Whelen's recipe is the best, and is given here: 6 ounces stronger ammonia, 4 ounces water, 1 ounce ammonium persulphate, 200 grains ammonium carbonate. Powder the carbonate and persulphate, and add the water and stronger ammonia, stirring until the salts are dissolved. Keep in a bottle with glass or rubber stopper. It should be made up fresh as wanted and not kept over two weeks. To use this in a lever action rifle you would first get a rubber cork to fit snugly into the chamber, so as to keep the ammonia out of the action. Fill barrel with solution from the muzzle, let stand half an hour, pour out, and finish cleaning with flannel patches moistened with stronger ammonia (28% gas), shoved through on a cleaning rod. Thoroughly dry by running through clean patches, and then oil with a rag soaked in some good gun oil. To restore a rusted barrel the same solution is used, alternating with scrubbing by the brass scratch brush. The bore is then scrubbed with the rust remover grease sold at the gun stores, and this is finally cleaned out and the bore oiled. It should show clean and clear.

The test of all cleaning is shooting the weapon again. If you have neglected it, or your cleaning is of the lick-and-a-promise order, it will show up in the rifle's groups. Some rifle steels, notably Winchester, stand a great deal of abuse and still shoot well, in the writer's experience. Smokeless powders are particularly hard on the .22 cat rifle tribe. If not cleaned after shooting, the "wild" groups that will be made are simply unbelievable. I have seen a dirty .22 that could not hit a blue rock pigeon at fifteen yards!

As for cleaning rods, I have three for the rifles: a plain hickory rod for the .35, a jointed brass rod for the .22's and the .32-20, and a brass scrubber with rope ends and a brass barrel weight to feed down from the muzzle for camp. This one goes in the ditty bag on the trail, together with a folding triple-blade screwdriver, a broken-shell extractor, and a steel supplementary cartridge that takes the .380 auto Colt pistol cartridge in the .35 for small game.

While it is true that the present price of shotgun shells has dropped to $1.25 a box, some of us like to load our own, at that. To do this with any sort of satisfaction requires, first, that you "get organized." As to economy, loaded shells now cost five cents "per each," as dear old Unkel David would say, whereas if you load them yourself they cost 2¾ cents. This is figured on powder at 85 cents a pound, which will load 85 shells at 3 drams each (256 drams to the pound), and chilled shot at 15 cents a pound. Wads are now about $2 a thousand, and primers 35 cents a box of 100. Time was when primers were a simple matter, but now they are very complex. You used to drive out the primer and set in a Winchester 2½ and there was an end! Now each shell has a different kind, some the old anvil type, others like little .22 cartridges necked down. However, the first thing to do after coming in from the hunt is to decap all your empties, partly to prevent corrosion of the flame hole and sticking of the primer, and partly to get a sample of the primer, so as to match him in buying a new box of them.

I do not know what brass shells cost now. Papers come about two cents each, new; brass will no doubt have gone to five cents. I still have a big stock of them, 12-gauge, 2½-inch. There is hardly a gun chamber that they will not fit, as the standard shell length is 2⅞ inches when uncrimped. These brassies are the goods for steady reloading; their only objection is a tendency to diminish in numbers, due to bending them out of round when on the hurly-burly of a grouse hunt where rocks are plentiful and cheap. With them I have a shell board holding fifty. It consists of two walnut boards, 12 inches by 6 inches, hinged together at the back and provided with two hooks in front. The upper board is one inch thick, and has fifty shell holes 11-16 inch in diameter bored in it, five rows of ten shells each, $1\frac{1}{8}$ inches between centers in the ten row and $1\frac{1}{16}$ inches in the five row. The lower board has shallow recesses bored in it, 15-16 inch in diameter, to receive the shell heads, and the centers of these are countersunk to make a shallow well into which the knocked-out primers are to be dropped.

All right; the board is first filled with fifty empties, folded and hooked together. The decapping punch goes over the lot, driving out all the old primers. Board is unhooked and upper board turned over, when all the shells are recapped, not with the tongs type, which would require taking them all out, but with that recapper which slides over the shell head like a shell extractor, and indeed may be used as such. Board is again folded together, when all fifty shells stand with their mouths up to be powdered. The wads come next, put in with a short funnel which fits over the shell down to the wood; and then comes the shot and its card wad.

The holes for the shells should fit them closely, as in paper shells you have nothing but the wood from preventing the shells fattening out if rammed too hard. Brass shells require their own wads, as the standard gauge paper shell wads are too small to fit them.

This board is equally quick and good for paper shells, the only other operation being to open the soft mouth of each shell with a little wood cone. When this is done the funnel will not be required, *if* you go light on the ramming.

Really, it is in rifle shell reloading that the greatest economy comes in these days of ten-cent cartridges. A pound of powder will load 233 thirty-grain cartridges. As the average big-game load is from 25 to 35 grains, and the price of nitro rifle powders around $1.35 a can, it brings the powder expense down to about half a cent. There are 7,000 grains in a pound weight, so that out of a pound of lead in the dipper you can get about 28 250-grain bullets, making the cost of them come one-third cent each at ten-cent lead. The rest is primer and gas check cup expense, so that it will cost about a cent each to reload such a cartridge as the .30-30 or the .30 U. S., with a trifle more for the .35 Winchester. The Ideal No. 10 tool will handle most of the modern big-game cartridges. With it you should buy a dipper and melting pot, with castiron rim to let it set in the ordinary kitchen stove hole, which seems to have just about the right heat for making good bullets. You need the ladle or dipper because of its nozzle, which goes flat on the mould vent and gives you a pressure pour, which cannot be had out of an improvised kitchen spoon. This dipper should be kept *in* the

SHELL RELOADING BOARD

RIFLE RELOADING TOOLS AND SHELL CRIMPER

lead bath when not pouring, to keep its temperature the same as the lead. The mould must be almost as hot as the lead to get good bullets. A sure test is that the bullet should take several seconds to harden after being poured. When your mould is heated to the right point, keep the bullets coming in a batch, so as to pour a new one soon enough after each cooling to keep the temperature of the mould up. Occasionally it needs a touch of tallow or beeswax to keep the bullets from sticking to the mould. Knock them loose with a blow from a billy on the body of the mould, and keep the mould hinge oiled.

I never had much trouble, after the first few, in making a nice run of bullets. The rest of the re-loading process is quick and simple. Your used shells should be cleaned as soon as possible after firing by dropping them in a bottle with soapsuds and weak ammonia, rinsing out the powder residue and drying in a mild heat—of course decapping, so as to get rid of the old primer with its corrosive pocket. It is the scale residue left in a dirty shell that makes all the trouble in reloading, for it dis-places at least five grains of room meant for the powder. When you try to seat the bullet, it is no go. Apparently some powder has to be tipped out, and it *will* have to, too, if the bullet is to seat home, with consequent loss of velocity when you come to fire the cartridge. Wherefore be not lazy, but clean your shells if you expect to reload them!

On the reloading tool you will find a bullet sizing die, a capper and decapper, and a finishing die for forming the loaded shell so it will fit the chamber nicely. Also a dingus for opening the shell necks, which may be needed if your bullets are not going in the neck properly, but most shells come out of the rifle slightly expanded in the neck from the explosion.

On the base of your bullet goes the copper gas check cup. It is a little, inexpensive thing, but if you have any regard for your rifling do not omit it. In our great gun firing in the navy the erosion due to each shot is all figured out in tables, so we know from the life of the gun just how much yardage short to allow for the erosion that has already taken place. Well, in rifle shooting this erosion is just as important, and it is best kept down by a gas check cup. A pure lead base will melt and fray around the edges, due to the white-hot gases behind it. This cup is to protect the base.

My own experience with reloading rifle shells has been a pleasurable sort of puttering, by no means the mystery or mess of hard feelings that sportsmen seem to think it will be. If you want to become a good shot, practice is the only thing that will do it, and your own reloading will give you that, cheap. It is a perfectly legitimate and commendable activity of the Sportsman's Workshop, I'll say!

CHAPTER VIII

Rod Repairing and Lure Making

THE tackle department of the sportsman's workshop will have two main concerns: the repair of rods and reels, and the making of tackles and lures. All of us who do much fishing need not be reminded of the number of lures we lost on each long trip of the season. Our floating bass baits got snagged beyond recovery, or cast off into the forest by some backlash, never to be found, and our spoon lures one by one came to grief, hooked in rock crevices, into lily pad stems and brush snags. At present prices of any and all lures, enough of them to last out a week's trip will cost more than the trip, so that we, perforce, take to making our own in the shop—which is good fun and not half so hard as it sounds.

As to rods and reels, they *will* come through the season with frayed wrappings, war-worn varnish, broken joints, and lost tops; and the reels, especially the salt-water division, get gummed up with green rust, while the fresh-water ones are apt to come home with the rubber cheek plates nicked or broken, the handles bent or loose, and the quadruple multiplying ones slow from dirt or even bent out of true, which often happens to the kind made of a shell of metal punched out to form the frame.

ROD REPAIRING AND LURE MAKING

So along about February we get out the fishing togs and see what ails each and every one of them. Here is a boat rod that was put away last season with its butt and second joint gummed together so that two strong men and a horse couldn't get it apart again. *Of course* it seized the occasion to spring itself out of straight. The butt joint is all right, but the second—a dog's tail is straighter! First, to get it apart. Don't put it in a vise and proceed to ruin it by twisting the ferrule with a pipe wrench. Just run a turn of kerosene around the rim of the ferrule and let it stand a day or so to think it over, adding a drop of kerosene again whenever you notice it needs it. My word for it, in two days at most that joint will come apart with the first strong endwise pull. To straighten the bent section, lay it on a board and drive in two nails near the ends. Bend straight—and a bittock more—by hand, and secure with a third nail. When you take it off a week later it will be straight or near enough so to complete the process by hanging up with a heavy weight attached to the bottom.

Overhauling the fly rod, one tip has lost its top, and all the joints have frayed sections here and there. Your tackle repair drawer will have the silk rod-winding spools of the colors you use. Get out the right spool and one of your old safety razor blades treasured up for rod work, and cut off the frayed wrapping entire with a slit down its length. Now to wind on the new one. The simplest rod lathe that I know of is two glass ice-water pitchers, set up on the bench with the rod joint passing through the handles of the pitchers. With this scheme the rod is turned with the right hand, its fingernails snugging the turns so that they lie flat side by side with no bunching and no open cracks, while the left hand feeds the thread off the spool at a tension. Such a wrapping is begun by winding over the end of the thread laid flat on the rod, and completed by making out a loop and winding over the loop for three or four turns, when the thread end is pushed through the loop and pulled taut, thus making an invisible knot. After these wrappings are on they will all need three or four coats of color fixer, which is collodion and banana oil in equal parts, bought from your druggist's. Without it the silk will surely turn dark and muddy when the varnish comes on. If the varnish already on the rod is in good shape, all the new wrappings will need is a single coat of new varnish, followed by another on the whole joint. We use spar or Valspar varnish, thinned out with a little alcohol. Your main concern will be to do the varnishing in some room where there is, and will be, no floating dust, and not to put on a new coat until the other is thoroughly dry; that is, so dry that no thumbmark will show when you press on it. If you put it on too soon the new coat melts the under one and the whole business gums up. The brush to do it with must be the finest you can buy, a sable brush that will not leave hairs and streaks.

Often a whole new rod-wrapping job comes up; in our shop many of them, for "B. M." is a professional at it, making all his own rods, repairing mine, and making up new ones from a score of old butts and tips and joints that abound in the dark recesses of the store closet. I had a green-heart surf rod that was stiff and logy and exceedingly difficult to cast without getting a backlash, as it had no life and whip. B. M., who had just finished a beautiful surf rod of his own, looked mine over and declared that it needed rebuilding from the ground up. It had a wrapping every inch, which not only made it *look* heavy and clumsy to a degree, but so bound the wood fibers as to take all the resiliency out of the rod. With a razor blade all these came off in a jiffy, also both upper guides and the top. The rod was then scraped down with an old blade, following with a rubbing of steel wool until we had the original grain. Testing its bend, B. M. decided on a removal of enough wood, from the ferrule down to about half the length of the tip, to give that long bend that is needed for a good surf rod, *not* the tight bend up near the top that you will find on poorly designed rods. A good test of a surf-rod tip is to hold it out with the left hand and strike it a smart blow with the palm of your right hand about one-third its length from the butt. It should vibrate smartly over its whole length for at least a second.

A single pair of agates was then put on, twenty inches from the top. To make a handsome job of this, he put on two green wrappings, with black edgings and yellow center line and yellow ends, followed by three narrow yellow rings about half an inch apart at each end, and over this was put the guides opposite the yellow centerline, and wrapped on with black silk, winding always *toward* the agate. This color scheme was repeated below the top and above the ferrule, and once again about midway between the ferrule and the guides. That was all the wrapping that went on the rod. Four coats of collodion and banana oil went on these, and then the varnish, taking several weeks to get on four coats of it, and rubbing down with steel wool after each coat to smooth down pimples and brush roughness in the surface. A reversible agate top completed the rod.

Before the war a good greenheart rod cost about $25. B. M. made his own at a cost of about $14, as follows: From Vom Hofe, in New York, he bought a greenheart tip with ferrule, 6 foot, 12 ounce, for $5. A Jersey spring butt, of betha-bara, with reel seat and buttpiece complete cost $5 more. Four agate guides and a reversible top stood him $3, and he was ready to assemble the rod, put on the wrappings as described above, and var-nish. In this rod he used the two-guide mounting, with guides 10 inches and 22 inches from the top, respectively. For ornament green cylinders with red borders and yellow center line and double yellow outer rings was used as the color scheme, one be-tween the two guides pairs and three between the lower pair and the ferrule. This tip came with a rattan-wound forward grip in front of the ferrule. It made a fine, handsome rod when finished, and always beat mine for ease and distance of casting.

During the winter our overheated houses have a great way of causing the cement in rod ferrules to perish, so that spring finds a good many of them loose when you put the rod together. The main difficulty about ferrules is to get them back on

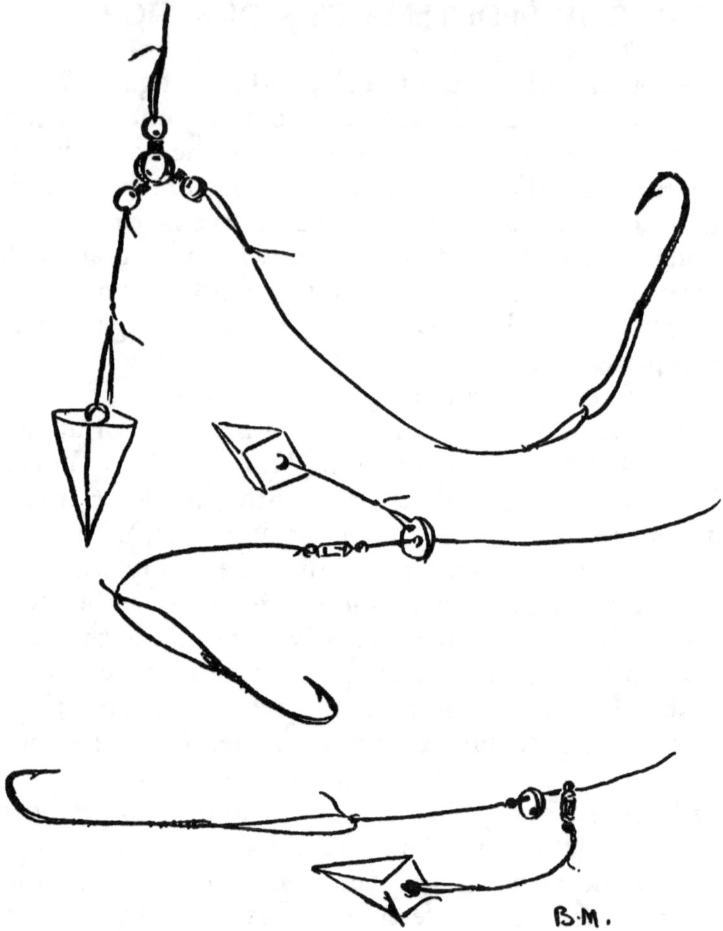

SALT WATER TACKLES

HOW TO MAKE AN INVISIBLE KNOT

straight again, so that the rod will not be full of dog's tails when put together. All the old cement should be carefully scraped and cleaned from wood and the inside of the ferrule. To put on a female ferrule it had best be first set on the male so that your eye has a chance to see that the joint is on straight before the cement sets. The rod and ferrule should both be warmed, and then the rod covered with fresh ferrule cement and the metal shoved over it. Try it for trueness with your eye, and either straighten by hand or take apart and do over again if it refuses to come in a straight line with the next joint. If there is a ferrule pin, drill a new hole for it with a fine awl before driving in the pin.

In scraping the varnish from split bamboo rods, be careful not to cut into the enamel of the bamboo itself. Friend Westervelt advises holding the razor blade flat for this purpose. We use it like a draw scraper, watching that we do not take off anything but varnish. It is a good plan to have some extra snake guides of three sizes in the tackle repair drawer, as more than one promising job has been halted by a snake guide dropped and lost beyond finding—probably making its escape down an expectant crack in the floor! The same applies to spare agates for brass rods, trumpets for boat rods, and at least one large top for the surf fellows; for an agate top once cracked will fray any amount of good line and is hopeless. For ferrule cement I prefer the kind that has to be heated to make it liquid. This can be done with even a single match out on the stream or beach, and the part is loosened by hand and either replaced or fixed. It is often just as important to get a top off easily as to get it on!

Reel repairs are principally oiling and cleaning. A set of screwdrivers that will fit in the slots of all the screws in your reels is the first thing to look to. No use spoiling a screw head irrevocably with a driver blade too big to fit the slot, or too small to grip clear across the head. Taking your bass reel apart, you will find a remarkable mixture of grease, dirt, dust, and fine metal-fouling in its pinion teeth. The reel has spun thousands of times during your fishing trip, and has industriously ground up all the impurities that filtered in through the case, until it now will hardly spin six seconds, whereas it ought to spin thirty-two on a single whirl. Take off the pinions and clean out each tooth carefully with a soft rag and a wooden pick point. Drop the whole thing in gasoline and wash it about. Clean off, put back, and oil with a light machine oil, and the reel will be back to pristine spinning power. The drags and clicks generally need cleaning and overhauling, and perhaps you will seize the occasion to put on that cork drum which you have been promising yourself—in these days of $2.50 bass lines!

Trout reels seldom give much trouble, being so "mighty" simple. In eight years the only thing that has happened to mine is one rubber cheek broken from its securing pin on the reel seat, by being dropped on the floor by some thumb-fingered dub. Fixed, by securing the pin to the next stanchion on both sides with three turns of fine wire. This held the rubber cheek pieces down in their broken holes and will answer—for a trout reel.

The salt-water reels are the ones that will give you many a fine surprise. Mine was taken out "as is," after the war was over and we were free to go fishing again. At the very first cast she set her automatic drag so tight that the handle could hardly be forced over. The unlocking pin for the take-apart mechanism was gummed fast with green rust, so that she could not be taken apart. There was no oilcan in the tackle box, either. In desperation I cast again, a mighty swipe which put the automatic drag permanently out of business; but it freed the spool and I went on fishing. Arrived home, I took the reel apart in some trepidation, expecting at least to find some ground-up disc or wheel that would have to be replaced from the factory. The least screwdriver, a little fellow with $\frac{1}{8}$-inch blade, was needed to back out the four stanchion screws, after which the rubber cheek plate was lifted out of its recess. And then—what ho, men!—there was nothing to it! The automatic drag sets with a hook, pushed out by a spring from the plate button and engaging a notch in the drag disc. This hook was stuck fast with sand and green rust. Push out, push in, Button! Neither moved the hook, the spring not being strong enough to free it. All it needed was cleaning, so that the hook would be free to move once more. Also tightening up the drag tension. *Of course* I took the whole drag mechanism apart, and got it together again with every single piece upside down, but as it obviously wouldn't work I fell to studying it and soon got at the principle of the thing. There are two spring plates and a disc plate, the latter with two notches in it to engage the set hook. A nut on the reel shaft puts a pressure on the disc, which, through the two spring plates, bears on the inside flange of the reel drum. As the hook is attached to the reel cheek piece, as soon as it engages the disc there is a tension between the drum and the fixed cheek piece of the reel. That is all there is *to* the automatic drag! You can adjust the tension to any amount required by setting up on the nut.

I never had any trouble with my bass reels except one, a punched frame take-apart reel, which came out of the trunk warped beyond recovery. We took off the ends of this reel and spent an evening trying to take the skew out of the frame and get the ends round enough to pass the drum flanges without touching, but in vain. No home tools will do this work to the thousandth's accuracy required for a clean-running fit. As it was B. M.'s only bass reel and we were a hundred miles from anywhere, we had to take turns using my stanchion type reel. Yet the other had not received any rougher usage than my reels usually get on dozens of trips. The factory fixed this reel for me later, without charge —as well they might!

I have seen any number of designs for rod-winding lathes, and am of the opinion that, for a single worker, two V-notch end rests and a movable center rest to put near the place where the wrapping is going on, is the most workable form of rod-winding "lathe." You need both hands to manipulate the wrapping turns, the right hand also revolving the rod. A means for foot-power turning of the rod is the best solution. The standard hardware store buffer head, with grooved wheel and two threads for a chuck and a polishing wheel bushing, make the best bench lathe for winding rods. Driving it will be a grooved wheel and treadle, which can be picked up at a junk or second-hand furniture dealer's and attached below your work table. On it there should be a small grooved wheel about the same size as the one in the buffer head, for a rod must turn over slowly, not spin, as it would do with the big flywheel. Then, in using the head as a drill or a turning lathe, you take off the rod-winding belt and put on the large one, to go around the rim of the flywheel like a sewing machine or jigsaw wheel.

The art of lure making is one that had little attention from the angling fraternity when good spinners and artificial baits were made up at prices that made no appreciable hole in one's expense account for a trip. But now!—a single look at the tackle-store counters shows an astonishing advance in the prices of these commodities. We simply *must* have enough lures to last out a trip, ten spinners, half a dozen "plugs," and five large red flies to use with pork minnows and chunks. One by one these get lost during the days' casting, until mighty few are left for the next trip. To buy a new set will cost more than the grub and car fare of the trip itself, wherefore we turn to the shop for relief. For materials we need brass wire of about 18 gauge, beads, nickel eyelets from a package of them bought at the ten-cent store, feathers, and spoons. These latter have caused many to hesitate, but as a matter of fact you have an inexhaustible supply of them in your old brass pistol and rifle cartridges. A pair of tin smith's shears is the only tool needed. Cut down the cylinder of the cartridge until about ¼ of an inch from the base, turn, and cut around the cartridge, and you have a nice sheet of brass, big enough for a one-inch spoon, from an empty old .38 pistol cartridge. The sheet is curved and springy, also dirty inside. Anneal it by holding in a blue gas flame for a moment, until it glows cherry-red. When cool it will be pliable to your fingers, and it cuts as easy as paper. For a bright brass finish simply polish on the buffer, daub over with banana oil and repolish, when you get a rust-proof finish. To silver them, dissolve a globule of quick-silver in a mixture of two-thirds hydrochloric acid and one-third nitric and dip the spoons in the mixture, one at a time to prevent undue generation of heat. They will come out with a mirror finish.

To make up spinners the basic elements are a piece of brass wire, bent into a long turn, with a catch around the shank in which the hook is to be hung; a bead, or a few of them, as a base on which the spoon is to twirl; the eye part of a hook-and-eye, with its eyes turned flat so as to slip over the wire and carry the spoon in its U; and, finally, the finishing eye turned in the end of the brass wire, in which the line is to be made fast. That is all there is to making a spinner. For double spoons use a longer wire, two eyes, and enough beads to space them properly. In making up Rangely spinners a single hook is hung in the bend of the wire and the hook is spun with red or green silk, with gray rooster's hackles or any other feathers that you have found killing, tied in behind the eye of the hook. For bass and pike spinners, a treble hook with red, gray, and white feathers tied at the upper part of the shank, a five-inch wire, and one or two brass 1¼-inch spoons will do fine. ·

For pork-rind baits I get a set of 6–0 hooks and secure over the shank of each a long-eared and slotted sinker weighing about ½ ounce. This is wrapped over with red thread, and a red feather tied on with its rib jutting up toward the hook point to make it weedless. Beginning with the hook eye, I put on a split ring, a swivel, another split ring and a second swivel. In the second split ring is hung a nickel or brass spoon about 1½ inches long. The pork minnow, 3 inches long, with tail split up 1 inch, is hung in the bend of the big hook, and the revolutions of the spoon make the minnow wiggle as it is reeled back to the boat. A mighty killing rig, in most lily-pad lakes. To make it effective for pickerel, hang a treble hook in the bend of the big one and stick one point of it through the side of the pork minnow.

As for artificial plug lures, you will have in the shop red and white enamel paint for refurbishing your battered ones, spare treble hooks and small screweyes to attach them with. To make up a plug bait, a white body with red head or throat seems the most attractive to bass. If the front face is cut flat, on a slant, the bait will dive and wobble. If you have the treble hook and screweye you can even make a bait in camp by whittling a crooked holly stick, anything that is white, tying your line a bit back of the head, and making the front face a slant. With the hook hung in the

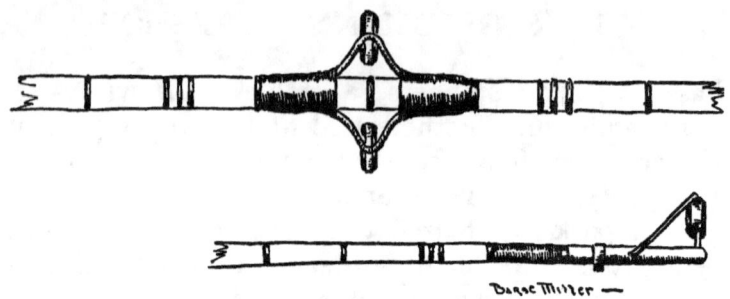

SALT WATER ROD WINDINGS

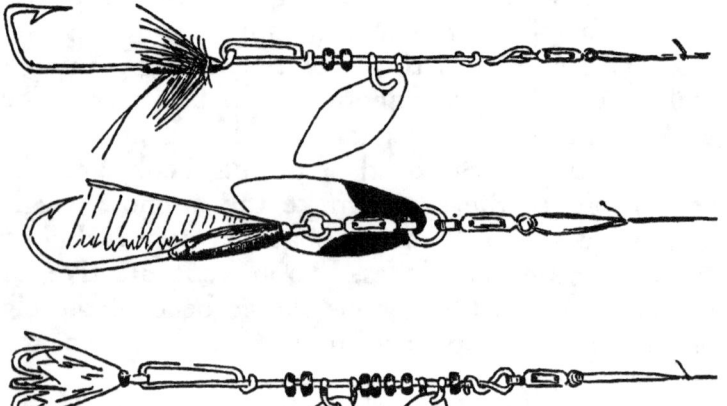

LURES AND SPINNERS

125

throat it will catch bass, and is the better for a tail-hook for pickerel.

It is the heavier-than-water lures, however, that one loses. It is seldom that a floating lure is snagged beyond recovery. What they principally need is repainting, so as to keep them bright and fresh. In preparing for a salt-water trip the shop will need to make up half a dozen standard tackles, consisting of a bronze three-way swivel, a leader of bronze picture wire two feet long, with an eye for the hook snell in one end of it, and 4-ounce pyramid sinkers attached to the lower swivel eye with a 6-inch length of line with two bowline loops in it. For channel bass a ¼-inch rawhide loop, with the sinker line attached to it and a bone button strung on the line below the loop has been found good, as it permits the fish to pick up the bait and run off with it without noticing the drag of the sinker and becoming suspicious. Another modification of the same rig is a large bone button with the line passing through one hole and the sinker line tied through the other. A split shot or even the knot on the end of the line will suffice to hold this in casting. It works the same way as the loop.

For bay weakfish and a light trout rod we find that an ordinary float bobber with the center stick taken out makes a good rig. The line is rove through the hole and a match stick or an office paper clip is put on where the depth below the float is right. When the fish strikes, the line is free to come back through the hole without the drag and inertia of the float. This is also good for still fishing for bass in deep water.

CHAPTER IX

Making Gun and Rod Cabinets

I'VE a whole lot of respect for the man who says, "Go to, now, let's make a"—well, anything he can't afford to buy, be it a sail or motor boat, a portable house or any other article where two-thirds of the price is in labor and profits. These winter days are great times for puttering and fussing about with a saw and a hammer; a busy season for the sportsman's workshop. A good many years ago when gun cabinets were selling for about $35—and not really artistic ones at that—I swore a round oath that my high-priced arsenal of guns should no longer be sequestered all winter in swaddled and oil-soaked rags and poked away out of sight in travel-worn leather gun cases. To be deprived of all sight of the beloved rifles and shotguns all winter was asking too, too much, yet if you hung them up on horns the beauties were sure to accumulate streaks of rust all along the tops of the barrels and the dust soon took the handsome gloss off lock, stock, and barrel.

Wherefore: "Go to, now, let's make a gun cabinet!" I wanted something handsome enough to take its place beside the best library or living-room furniture made; something that would show off my pets to best advantage, and something with plenty of drawers in it for tackle, camp duffle, shells, loading tools; everything that would spell OUTDOORS at me through the long winter evenings. There were three shotguns and three rifles to be taken care of; shell belts; boots; a little five-pound tent; a camp axe, and five gun cases. It seemed to me that polished black walnut with brass fittings and a hunter's green felt lining to the gun compartment would make a rather handsome piece of furniture, especially if it had a pair of plateglass doors in front so as to show off the polished artillery inside. And I couldn't see anything to admire in the folding table-board put in front of some cabinets. Not only would it cover the gunstocks and locks when down, but it would not give room enough for a really enjoyable shell-loading bee if used for that purpose as advertised. Then I wanted plenty of small drawers in it, at least a dozen, so it would not be hard to find anything when wanted.

There was a lot of fun planning these drawers. Taking the standard, 4 inches by 4 inches by 10 inches deep, you needed two 6 inches by 4 inches by 10 inches at the bottom on each side for shell crimpers and powder cans. Then you needed a drawer for wads, another for shot, another for shells, another for primers and loading tools, one for rifle loading set and rifle shells, a drawer for compass, small camp duffle, surgical kit, etc.; another for ditty bag and hunting knife; another sacred to reels, one for lines and flies, and one exclusively for hooks, sinkers, lures, and such small deer. Above the drawers ought to be a 10-inch space on each side for favorite outdoor textbooks, while under

the drawers the partition could come in a little to
make a space 5½ inches wide by 14 inches high on
each side. One of these would hold the tent in its
green denim covering and the other the shell belts
and outing boots. I next planned a shallow drawer
3 inches deep and the full width of the gun cabinet
to go under the gun rack, and in which to keep the
gun cases handy for field use. Having planned thus
far, the thing began to take definite shape in feet
and inches, so I set about building a cabinet 61
inches high, 12½ inches deep, and 28½ inches
wide, which would have a row of six 4-inch drawers
down each side and would hold six guns and two
rods in the central rack. Black walnut is rather
rich for a poor sportsman's pocketbook, but white
wood (tulip tree) grains beautifully, is easily worked,
and, when stained with any good clear black walnut
stain, will polish to look exactly like the real black
walnut. So I got out two ⅞-inch dressed planks of
white wood 5 feet 1 inch long by 12½ inches wide,
planed the edges and carved a simple English
Gothic arch out of the bottom to make a finish for
the feet on each side. Next the top and bottom
boards were sawed off the plank. The former is a
piece of 28-inch by 12½-inch by ⅞-inch, nailed
over the ends of the side planks with 10-d brads
and the bottom is 1¾ inches shorter, going in between the sides on concealed nail-strips. Another
board, exactly like the bottom, was put 3 inches
above it to form the bottom of the gun rack, but
this board was only 10 inches wide, so as to come
inside the cabinet doors.

I next bought some ½-inch planks of white

wood 10 inches wide and set up out of these the lower 5½-inch by 14-inch compartments on each side, following with the long drawer side partitions, running from the top of the cabinet down into the top board of the side compartments. Then there were days of fussing with the drawer partitions and making the drawers; particularly getting them so they would not stick, but finally every last one of the dozen slid back onto its stop like an angel. The bottom drawer was 3 inches by 26 inches by 10 inches, and upon its completion I was ready for the decorative work.

To begin with, the flat sides were anything but handsome, so to relieve their monotony I skirmished around in the moulding stock of a nearby carpenter shop and got out a lot of flat white wood moulding with cove and bead edge, the moulding being 1½ inches wide and ⅜ inch thick. This I ran around the sides of the cabinet, bringing it just under the cornice, and crossing below on the level with the bottom of the cabinet, so that the arch of the feet came below this trim. All the corners of it were, of course, mitered and it was fastened on the sides with concealed brads, flush with front and back faces. For a top cornice I used 2-inch O. G. moulding mitered around front and sides, and this in its turn was supported by a 1¼-inch corner trim of fancy pressed and beaded corner moulding. After sandpapering all over and sinking and puttying all brads, I gave the entire cabinet a coat of black walnut stain, through which the grain of the white wood showed beautifully. Then three coats of No. 1 carriage varnish, rubbing down each coat with No. O sandpaper, horsehair, and pumice stone and oil, and finally polish only. In this way I soon got a smooth, glossy oil finish all over it, and then put in the hunter's green felt lining of the gun compartment. To make the bottom racks for the gunstocks I concealed ¾-inch by ⅜-inch by 8¾-inch sleepers under the felt, and for the barrel racks I cut out two 2⅛-inch semi-circles, spaced 2½-inch centers for each gun. This was screwed to the back of the cabinet 3 feet 3 inches above the floor, and each semi-circle was lined with a strip of felt so as not to mar the precious gun barrels. The front doors of the cabinet were next made of 2-inch by ⅞-inch stock white pine frames 13 inches wide by 55 inches long. They were rabbeted to receive the panes of ⅛-inch glass, 10¼ inches by 52¼ inches, and then stained and polished. The glass was held in the rabbets by strips of ⅜-inch by 3/16-inch rock elm, also stained and polished, and secured by tiny brads so that the glasses can be taken out and packed in their own box whenever the gun cabinet has to go into a moving van.

It was now time to go after display, in the brass work of the hinges, latch and knobs of the drawers. The photographs will give some idea of how this looked. The drawer knobs are ⅞-inch diameter, of heavy brass, with knurled edges, and I had a dozen 2-inch circular flat pedestals turned out by a wood-lathe artist, which gave "some class" to the securing of the knobs to the drawers. I used altogether ten knobs for the 4-inch drawers, two ring handles for 6-inch drawers, two square plate handles for bottom drawer, four fancy hinges for cabinet doors; one fancy lock; two heavy brass hooks for revolvers and shell-belts, and top and bottom brass concealed bolts in cabinet doors. About $4 worth of fancy brass work. The rest of the cabinet did not cost over $5, all told, except the glass for the front doors, which came to $1.04. Lumber and sundries bill: 18 B. F. D2S, ⅞-inch white wood; 30 B. F., ½-inch white wood; 25 feet 1½ by ⅜-inch moulding; 6 feet 2 inches by ⅞-inch O. G. moulding; 6 feet 1½ inch pressed moulding; 22 feet 2 inch by ⅞-inch dressed joist; 2 yards hunters' green felt; can of walnut stain; 2 cans carriage varnish.

If a man is an all-around four-sided sportsman, his gun cabinet is sure to slowly but steadily fill up with beauty double shotguns and world-beater rifles, until there is a considerable overflow meeting in some corner of the den of fishing rods and other outdoor pieces of bric-à-brac which have been crowded out of the sacred precincts of the gun cabinet. This is one of those did-it-ever-happen-to-you's that *did* happen to me, and forced, in time, the inevitable query, Why not a rod cabinet? Here were seven homeless rods with their attendant reels, a whole menagerie of gaudy flies, wooden worms and wonder minnows, tackle and angling paraphernalia galore—and no fixed locus for any of them. And so a rod cabinet began to take shape in my thoughts. I had never seen one, nor do I believe there is such a thing on the market, but it seemed to me that such a cabinet should be arranged to hang all tips and second joints from some sort of curtain pole and ring device which would make them easy to get at; that all butts with their reels attached should be arranged around the interior, with spring clips to hold them in place, like those foreign cane racks, and that the cabinet should be tall enough to take one-piece bait casting rods and 6-foot surf rod tips without difficulty. Then there should be drawers for miscellaneous tackle, tin-lined compartments for trout, bass, and salmon flies, and a row of brass hooks for squids, spoons, tasseled minnows, and benighted plugs. The creel, nets, waders, and gaff belonged more properly with pack bags and camp gear outside of the rod cabinet, which I proposed should rival in glory and beauty the gun cabinet itself.

As for the treatment of the case, plain mission is the easiest to do, and yet be able to get a handsome finished effect with ordinary home tools and talent; so I chose this style with red oak for the panel boards and white for the four square posts which were to go at the corners. The construction of the cabinet is really a very simple matter. It calls for an oak back 12 inches wide by 5 feet 2 inches high, two oak sides 8 inches by 5 feet 2 inches and a top and bottom 12¾ inches by 8 inches. Nail these up with brads into a long, narrow box. Order from the mill 24 feet of 1½ inches by 1½ inches square white oak, dressed four sides, and make four posts 5 feet 6 inches long. Round over the tops neatly and nail them along the front and back of your box, forming thereby four square posts or columns at the corners. The nails should be brads, driven concealed from the inside of the box. Allow the two front posts to project ⅞ inch beyond the front edge of the cabinet, making a recess for the glass door. Now order some ½-inch white wood and make two drawers, one 6 inches deep by 6 inches high and 12 inches wide, and the other 6 inches deep by 3 inches high by 12 inches wide. You will note that they will come, when closed, 2 inches from the back of the cabinet, where you should nail a stop to prevent them going in any further. This 2-inch space in behind the drawers leaves room for your long one-piece rods and surf rod tips, which need the full height of the cabinet to go in at all. The upper 3-inch drawer will only need ½-inch by ½-inch by 8-inch strip runners under it, but the lower drawer wants a ½-inch by 8-inch by 10-inch bottom board, nailed in just above it for rod butts to rest upon. It must have round holes cut in the back to pass the butts of one-piece rods and long surf tips. Line the interior of the cabinet with dark red felt or leave it natural finish and stain with Colonial art finish, tobacco brown, or weathered oak, to suit your fancy. The stain is rubbed on with a rag and brings out the grain beautifully. All it then needs is rubbing down with furniture polish to acquire a truly "profesh" appearance. The door you had best order from some door and sash mill, as it is impossible for an amateur without machinery to get neat corners and muntin joints. The frame should be of white wood, 1½ inches by ⅞ inch stock. Lights, four 8 inches by 15 inches, plain panes, or, if you prefer diamond panes, the mill can get you up something of stock sizes, but it will cost a good deal more. If your cabinet is 5 feet 2 inches high inside, the door will need to be 5 feet 3¾ inches by 10¾ inches, allowing for ⅞-inch stock. Stain at the same time you do the cabinet. As to hardware, the less of it that is seen in mission design the better. Have your hinges small, ¾-inch by 1¼ inches, brass, butt pattern, countersunk flush into the wood, and the backs coming just flush with the face of the cabinet. The lock should be a small brass mortise lock with plain, inconspicuous keyhole, without any escutcheon.

Your cabinet is now ready for the rod fittings. For tips and second joints get some ¾-inch black walnut curtain poling, and cut two 8-inch pegs from it, which drive into the back board of the cabinet so that they will stick out horizontally into the interior of the cabinet. Place them 3 inches apart and 3½ inches from the sides of the cabinet, and of the height to swing clear your longest tip. Get brass curtain rings to fit the poles with a small brass hook dangling from each. The left-hand peg will hang a dozen tips and the right-hand the second joints. The latter will need small brass screweyes screwed into the stopper plugs to hang them up by, as it is essential that they hang down straight.

There remain the various butts. On each side you will have room for at least four. Turned and polished black walnut curtain pole sockets are the thing for a recess to hold the bottom ends of your butts, while a corresponding row of brass cane spring-clips, which you can get from any big hardware store, are what you want to hold the upper ends of the butts. Each one carries its reel attached, and as no two reels are at the same height, it is not difficult to get them all placed without interfering; and if you own a collection of marvelous minnows and thousand-hook centipedes you can display a row of twenty of them on brass hooks, screwed in just below the upper drawer all around the interior of the cabinet.

The *raison d'être* of the rod cabinet is the same as the gun cabinet—protection from deterioration and the placing of your pet rods where you can see them and dream over them in idle moments. Your delicate tips are not warped as they would be from a winter in the rod bag, nor are your beautiful rods poked away in some closet where rust doth corrupt and moths break through and steal, only to be taken out and looked at on rare occasions. Instead they are a continuous delight to the eye during the winter evenings in the den, and if any rod needs repairing you are reminded of it every time you glance at your cabinet. The cost of it, as I have described it, will not exceed $4 for lumber, hardware, felt, and stain.